Disavowal

Theory Redux series
Series editor: Laurent de Sutter

Published Titles

Disavowal

Alenka Zupančič

polity

The right of Alenka Zupančič to be identified as Author of this Work has been asserted in accordance with the UK Copyright, Designs and Patents Act 1988.

First published in 2024 by Polity Press

Polity Press
65 Bridge Street
Cambridge CB2 1UR, UK

Polity Press
111 River Street
Hoboken, NJ 07030, USA

ISBN-13: 978-1-5095-6119-3
ISBN-13: 978-1-5095-6120-9 (pb)

A catalogue record for this book is available from the British Library.

Library of Congress Control Number: 2023950628

Typeset in 12.5 on 15pt Adobe Garamond
by Cheshire Typesetting Ltd, Cuddington, Cheshire
Printed and bound in Great Britain by TJ Books Ltd, Padstow, Cornwall

The publisher has used its best endeavours to ensure that the URLs for external websites referred to in this book are correct and active at the time of going to press. However, the publisher has no responsibility for the websites and can make no guarantee that a site will remain live or that the content is or will remain appropriate.

Every effort has been made to trace all copyright holders, but if any have been overlooked the publisher will be pleased to include any necessary credits in any subsequent reprint or edition.

For further information on Polity, visit our website:
politybooks.com

Contents

Acknowledgements

This monograph is a result of the research programme P6-0014 'Conditions and Problems of Contemporary Philosophy' and two research projects: N6-0286 'Reality, Illusion, Fiction, Truth: A Preliminary Study' and J6-4623 'Conceptualizing the End: its Temporality, Dialectics, and Affective Dimension', which are funded by the Slovenian Research and Innovation Agency.

Introductory Remarks

A man says to his wife: 'If one of us dies, I shall move to Paris.'

Freud cites this joke in his text 'Thoughts for the Times on War and Death', first published in 1915. He uses it to illustrate his argument that we do not believe in our own death (this is true particularly of our unconscious mind) and that it is impossible to imagine our own death, for even when we do imagine it we are still there, present as spectators, not really dead. We *know* of course that death exists, and we also 'experience' it with others, with the pain and irreversibility that come when people close to us die. But this knowledge of death, and the capacity to talk rationally about death as natural, undeniable, and unavoidable, changes nothing about the fact that, 'in reality, however, . . . we behave as if it were otherwise.'[1] This formulation is the template for the notion of disavowal (*Verleugnung*), which Freud develops in a later essay on fetishism,[2] and for which Octave Mannoni has provided the most concise formula: 'I know well, but all the same. . . .'[3] As is clear from this formula, disavowal differs from denial; it doesn't deny facts but gladly announces knowing all about them, and then it goes on as before. It is the contention of this essay that (perverse) disavowal, which sustains some belief by means of ardently proclaiming the knowledge of the opposite, is becoming a predominant feature of our social and political life and goes well beyond personal psychology.

It seems we often wonder how it is possible that the project of enlightenment could end with a triumph of obscurantism – the rise of all sorts of strange beliefs, mistrust in science, populism that relies on anything but rational argumentation . . . Lacanian psychoanalysis offers an answer: it is not because dark forces and obscure drives have overpowered reason and won over knowledge and its evidence, but because reason and knowledge have never been without their own obscure and 'unreasonable' side. The contemporary social modality of disavowal is a *perverse form of reason*, of knowledge itself, and not a return of some archaic and obscure drive. The appeals to reason and to science tend to forget or ignore precisely that; mostly they end up in outraged frustration or else in arrogance, amazed and amused by the 'stupidity of people'. These appeals operate with a clear distinction between knowledge and belief and ignore the role that knowledge can play in sustaining the most obscure beliefs – which is precisely what the concept of disavowal helps us to understand.

At the same time, we should not fail to see to what extent the profound entanglement of science with contemporary forms of capitalism, with its progress and 'growth', induces a mistrust in science. 'Irrational' mistrust in science often has a displaced rationale; it appears as a displaced mistrust of capitalism, a denunciation of capitalism *by proxy*. And this is particularly the case when people are convinced that capitalism is the best or the only possible organization of social economy (and abhor all mention of something such as communism) yet at the same time live and experience the brutal and traumatic reality of this same social order.

The concept of disavowal describes our general social state of mind more accurately than, say, denial, which is the term we otherwise prefer to use to describe our non-confrontation with certain traumatic aspects of reality. Denial also exists, of course, and we will discuss its specificity as well as its connection to disavowal in the chapter on conspiracy theories. (Perverse) disavowal is far less extravagant, more reasonable. It claims to be 'well aware of the problem' and is indistinguishably fused with what we like to call the 'liberal mainstream', starting with its economic and political centres of power. Indeed, politically speaking, we seem to be caught in a macabre dance in which denial (often associated with 'populism'), on the one hand, and perverse disavowal (associated with the business-as-usual mainstream), on the other, constitute two principal and competing *political* options, each fuelling the other with their respective pathologies, responding mostly to each other rather than to any social reality.

This essay examines various facets of the concept of disavowal. It takes its conceptual starting point in Mannoni's seminal text and then ventures to articulate some of the important modifications that the functioning of disavowal undergoes in our contemporary social context. It also relates this discussion to some other concepts, such as certainty, anxiety, and deception, and explores the deeply ambiguous social role of conspiracy theories. The entire book is in dialogue with some of the key problems that corrode our present and does not shy away from attempting a rigorous conceptualization of what is at stake in these problems. The conceptual arc grows denser in the middle of the book, while the first and last parts have a looser texture.

I

Exposition:
Father, Can't You See I'm Burning?

One of the tropes or master signifiers that keeps emerging in the recent onslaught of various crises – which now already constitute something of a 'serial crisis' – is *nightmare*. This word, which was present particularly during the Covid pandemics, seems to lend itself well not only to other crises (economic crises, the Ukraine war, the energy crisis, the Middle East crisis, the climate crisis and its related extreme weather events . . .) but even more to their seriality, to the way they are hitting us one after another, faster than we can keep up. Gérard Wajcman made this point very nicely in his book on series:[1] the series form or format is not just an aesthetic or artistic phe-nomenon. Rather, it is the language of the world such as it is: a world in crisis. Series is a form of crisis.

If 'nightmare' seems affectively to capture this series-as-crisis, it is also a good place to start our discussion. There is a dream – a nightmare – that Freud discusses very briefly in *The Interpretation of Dreams*, and which gained more deserved attention and fame because of Lacan's reading of it in his Seminar XI, *The Four Fundamental Concepts of Psychoanalysis*. It seems that its structural logic could hardly be more timely. Here is Freud's rendering of the dream and of its circumstances:

A father had been watching beside his child's sick-bed for days and nights on end. After the child had died, he went into the next room to lie down, but left the door open so that he could see from his bedroom into the room in which his child's body was laid out, with tall candles standing round it. An old man had been engaged to keep watch over it, and sat beside the body murmuring prayers. After a few hours' sleep the father had a dream that *his child was standing beside his bed, caught him by the arm and whispered to him reproachfully: 'Father, don't you see I'm burning?'* He woke up, noticed a bright glare of light from the next room, hurried into it and found the old watchman had dropped off to sleep and that the wrappings and one of the arms of his beloved child's dead body had been burned by a lighted candle that had fallen on them.[2]

The key question is, of course, where to situate the real that woke the father up. Strangely, Freud discusses this dream only very briefly, and just as an example of how a dream can satisfy the need to prolong sleep. The fire (in reality) should wake the father up, but the exhaustion made him incorporate fire in the content of his dreams so that he was able to continue to sleep. But then another, extraordinary thing happens, which Freud doesn't discuss in his account: something appears, takes place *within this fire dream itself*, something the violence and pain of which nevertheless wakes the father up, namely his son's words: *Father, don't you see I'm burning?*

As Lacan puts it in his commentary on this dream, 'this sentence is itself a firebrand – of itself it brings fire where it falls – and one cannot see what is burning, for the flames blind us to the fact that the fire bears on the *Unterlegt*, on the *Untertragen*, on the real.'[3]

What wakes the father up is not simply the reality of fire but what this reality is able to trigger, to represent, to smuggle into the dream as the burning real of his son's death, and of the father's inability to do anything about it, to perhaps prevent it. It is this other real that ultimately wakes the father up, the real that possibly includes many other difficult facets of their father–son relationship. And if up to a certain point the dream may indeed be said to satisfy the need to prolong sleep, the configuration changes at this point, and dramatically so. The dream comes up with something traumatic enough to achieve what the real fire was not able to do: to wake the father up. The situation is thus reversed. It is no longer that the fire is incorporated in the dream so that the father is able to continue to sleep; rather, what takes place in the dream wakes the father up, *so that he can go on dreaming*. Namely, and as also provocatively suggested by Lacan, it often happens with dreams that *we wake up so as to go on dreaming*. This is particularly true for nightmares, and generally true for the dreams in which a real appears that is more real, more traumatic and shattering than our everyday reality. So, in response we wake up (to reality), and proclaim to be awake, in order to be able to continue to dream – that is, to continue to exist more or less untouched, unscathed by the real that has just appeared. Which is why the real nightmare is precisely one from which we cannot wake up. A nightmare is defined not only, or not simply, by its traumatic content but by the fact that we cannot wake up (and escape to reality). The traumatic real is there, and it should make us wake up so as to escape it, but for some reason(s) this is prevented from happening: we are stuck with it.

Could we not say that many of the current crises have the same structure as the dream discussed above? Not just because we experience them as painful and 'nightmarish' but for two much more precise and specific reasons:

1. They confront us with something more than just the immediate crisis (the fire we need to put out), with something profoundly disturbing and disturbed in our social, ecological, political way of being. In other words, they point to another fire within the fire, which we would also need to consider and confront. (Devastating fires that are taking place more and more often all across the globe, from

Canada to Greece, Hawaii and California, to take just a few recent examples, are both a very direct and very metaphorical rendering of this: apart from the fire that needs to be extinguished in each case, there is yet another fire – climate change – that keeps on burning.)

2. What we tend to do in this double- or cross-fire is precisely that we readily wake up – so as to be able to go on dreaming, to forget about the fire that bears on the real. Extinguishing the fire at hand, attending to its victims (or not, if they are not the right kind of victims), is us waking up. But while this usually fails to lead much further, in the direction of also dealing with the fire within the fire, it also allows us to ignore the other fire (for 'this is not the right time'; but then it never is – there is always another emergency to attend to). The zeal with which we jump up and react, reach out, express concern, outrage, solidarity, is of course laudable, but it also often carries in itself a surplus dimension of serving its own purpose, as well as the purpose of disavowing the fire that bears on the real in the Lacanian sense. Attending to this other fire is obviously not an easy task, and it can happen only in a collective way, which

makes it all the more difficult to imagine. From possible and difficult political imagination we thus, rather, return to the 'real world', to the 'real problems' of 'real people', as the usual rhetoric has it, and this remains firmly within the given. Yet what is thus cut off is precisely the possibility that political imagination (and a new, substantially different political organization based on it) would *in fact* attend to the 'real problems' of 'real people'.

Here resides the profound ambiguity in 'waking up' and concerning everything that this trope evokes. If we look at the series of contemporary crises, are we not dealing in all these cases, and in spite of their obvious differences, with a situation where we wake up so as to be able to continue to dream? Saved by the bell, saved by the alarm clock, saved by 'harsh reality'? Each time we tend to proclaim that what hits us is a complete 'game changer', that we have finally woken up, yet at the same time we go on mostly as before, as if nothing has really happened, or else we (want to) return to some anterior state. There are certainly many declarations and a lot of commotion surrounding this 'waking up', but in the midst of all this commotion we just seem to go on dreaming.

Let's take the example of climate change: allegedly in this respect as well, we have 'woken up'. But how does this manifest, mostly? There is a lot of verbal, formal acknowledging of the crisis (I don't think denial is the predominant response any more, and we'll return to that); a whole newspeak is emerging out of this awareness ('green transition', 'green economy', 'sustainability'); there is lots of commotion, there are conferences, declarations ... And there is no doubt that, generally speaking, most people do take climate change more seriously than they did, say, ten or fifteen years ago. But still: faced with the numbers and very reliable scientific calculations, as well as with devastating events around us (extreme weather, fires, floods . . .), we mostly seem to go on dreaming in the midst, and with the help, of all this commotion. 'Growth' still remains the master signifier of our economy. The key word seems to be 'adaptation'. We keep hearing that 'we need to adapt to the new reality' – but what exactly does this mean? We do indeed seem to be able to adapt to almost everything, but is this really the best path to take? It is relatively easy to adapt or get used to a new reality. What is much more difficult is to 'tarry with the real', with the fire within the fire, to take into account the impossible real of what is happening and mobilize, organize on the grounds of its truth. As Lacan also perspicuously put it: 'We get used to reality. The truth [which also emerges with and from every crisis] we repress.'[4]

Repress, or else disavow, which is a slightly different thing, or a very particular modality of repression. What in fact is the difference between repression and disavowal? We could formulate it in simple topological terms. Repression effectually implies two dimensions or two levels, our reality and another level where what is pushed out, 'repressed' from our reality, exists: what is repressed no longer constitutes part of our reality. Disavowal, on the other hand, is one-dimensional, in the sense that what is disavowed does not disappear from reality: it is still there, on the same level, part of our reality (everything is out in the open – we know it well, and say so). So, disavowal doesn't make something disappear; rather, it changes, affects the nature and meaning of this something. We could say that it de-realizes it. It affects its character of the

real, as real – that is, as an *extra-ordinary*, surprising, shattering bit of our reality. When you
perceive or learn about something and disavow
it, it is because this something has the capacity to change reality for you; it is not just '*any*
stupid thing' from this reality. The same could
be said for repression, of course. But whereas
repression preserves the extra-ordinary character
of that *thing* by pushing it out of our ordinary
reality, disavowal keeps it as part of reality, yet
changes its character. We could thus say that
disavowal consists in making – what is for me,
and perhaps not only for me – an extraordinary,
'game-changing' fact, an ordinary fact – *but still
a fact*. What is disavowed is its shattering, game-
changing dimension and not simply its fact, or
its occurring. Perhaps it is this that we like to
refer to as a post-factual world: not that there are
no more facts – on the contrary, there are only
facts around – yet they are 'just facts' and no
longer carry any weight of the real.

And it is worth emphasizing that the status quo
maintained in this way does not mean simply
that everything stays the same but also that even
the most drastic changes (for the worse) do not
really get to us. 'Adapting effectively to the new

reality' can be part of the status quo. And so can numerous forms of catastrophism and fascination with the apocalypse, with various disasters and predictions of doom, with the spectacle of it. Far from being the opposite of disavowal, this kind of catastrophism is an important part of its contemporary functioning. The end of the world, for example, acts as a kind of spectacular backdrop, a coulisse, a stage on which we can simultaneously go on with our business as usual. More often than not the images of the apocalypse are but a phantasmatic screen that screens (and protects us from) the actual 'apocalypse' that is already going on and is not waiting for us somewhere in the future.

Disavowal and denial are not the only modalities of avoiding, circumventing some deeply upsetting real. There is also déjà vu or false memory, which actually comes very close to disavowal in the way it invokes knowledge ('Oh, nothing really new about this, we have seen this many times before!' – disavowing in this way the *unprecedented* character of what is happening).

In his discussion of the phenomenon of so-called *fausse reconnaissance* (false memory), Freud starts by pointing out how 'It not infrequently happens in the course of an analytic treatment that the patient, after reporting some fact that he has remembered, will go on to say: "*But I've told you that already*" – while the analyst himself feels sure that this is the first time he has heard the story.'[5] What then is the logic at stake in the phenomenon of false memory or déjà vu? This is how we might put it to make the point as clear as possible: something that has just arisen and is of traumatic/disruptive nature is intercepted (and de-realized) by a precipitate knowledge/ recognition of it; we look at it as belonging to some other time (or temporality). We are looking straight at the traumatic thing (it is right there, *in front of our eyes*, fully acknowledged), yet we see it as coming from far away, as strange and indifferent. The *fausse reconnaissance* thus paradoxically maintains the unfamiliar (strange, indifferent) character of what appeared by means of the very *feeling of recognition* and familiarity. It's already known and 'boring' before its meaning can even register. We might also say that it maintains this indifferent character by means of cutting the thing from its possible articulation as presence in reality: for this articulation appears already for the first time as its own memory.

Déjà vu also functions as a powerful *social form* of disavowal – that is, disavowal as built in the very foundations of our objective socio-economic relations, as well as in the ideology that sustains them.[6]

As social rather than just individual structure, disavowal also undergoes some important permutations, which can be resumed briefly as follows: *knowledge* about some traumatic reality (the 'I know well') gets strangely redoubled or split and *itself* starts playing the role of the object fetish that protects us against this traumatic reality. 'Knowledge' thus adopts a new and different role: it is no longer simply something to be disavowed but – paradoxically – something that can help us disavow (the real of this same knowledge). We'll discuss this in more detail in the next chapter.

We often hear that contemporary biopolitics reduces us to 'bare life', or that it enslaves us by making us hostages to mere survival. I am not sure that this is really the case. There is little evidence that we really care that much about our survival; rather, we seem to be caught up in a deeply (self-)destructive carnival in which we enjoy the spectacle of possibly dying and disappearing. Lives do not really matter (except rhetorically), or actually only some lives matter. Rather than being survivalists, we seem to be caught in a kind of 'crazy heroism': we would – quite literally – rather die than let ourselves be scared to death by what we are facing. We are more afraid of something 'scaring the shit out of us' than of actually dying.

Should we then conclude, with Günther Anders, that we need to increase our capacity for fear, to stop fearing fear and have the courage to be frightened?[7] Well, perhaps, but things are a bit more complicated than that. It is not certain that fearing the fear itself is the most precise diagnosis of our state of mind. At least in the present context, we may be a bit too quick in evading another significant social dimension of fear, namely the fear of deception, of being perhaps purposely and systematically deceived. This comes particularly to the fore in conspiracy theories but is by no means restricted to them. Not being naïve, or anybody's fool, often seems to be our top priority. Perhaps we should put it like this: we are concerned much more with the possibility of a *deception/illusion* (about some real) than with this real itself and its traumatic dimension. And, while compared to the 'fear of fear', this fear of deception may seem more superficial or anecdotal, merely psychological and lacking in depth. We will show in the next chapter that this is not necessarily so, and that the fear of deception can in fact be connected to a *profound ontological anxiety*. Here we might recall a very lucid remark that Clément Rosset makes in his analysis of the double, or the *Doppelgänger*, which can be seen as a figure of a false and deceptive other-me. If something like my double appears, we are dealing not with two constituted rival ontological entities (me and my double) but, rather, with something that induces a doubt in the original – me – as an ontological entity. Rosset reverses the standard diagnosis of Otto Rank, who linked the anxiety in the face of a double to our primordial fear of death. We usually consider the reality of the double to be 'better' than ours – and in this sense it can indeed seem that the double represents an immortal instance in relation to the subject (which is Rank's thesis). However, the real source of our anxiety is not simply our future death but, above all, the possibility of our (present) non-reality and non-existence, the fact that *it could be that we are not*. As Rosset puts it: it wouldn't be so hard to die if we knew for sure that we have at least lived; but it is precisely this life, as perishable as it is, that the subject starts to doubt in the cases of 'split personality' or the appearance of a double. This anxiety goes deeper than a fear of death. In the ill-fated couple in which I am united with a phantom other, the real is not on my side but, rather, on the side of the phantom: it is not the other that redoubles me; it is instead that I am the other's double.[8]

Something similar can be said to be in play with the fear of deception: the implications of what appears to be fear of looking foolish and naïve are reaching all the way to the core of our very (past and present) being. This can explain to some extent why the prospect of our future (even if imminent) death seems less scary than the idea of our existence, our being as it is now, possibly constituting a scam – because it bears on our present (and past) reality rather than on our future reality. To paraphrase Rosset: to perish in the future would at least confirm that we have lived. The anxiety relating to deception can be much more visceral. At the same time, it looks as if acute awareness, proclaimed knowledge of deception, can somehow provide a paradoxical life jacket maintaining us in being . . .

2

Conceptual Niceties

In 1964 Octave Mannoni published in *Les Temps modernes* what is still considered a seminal psychoanalytic text on disavowal. In 1969 this was republished as part of his book *Clefs pour l'Imaginaire, ou l'Autre Scène*. Its title succinctly spells out the core formula of disavowal: *Je sais bien, mais quand même*, 'I know well, but all the same. . . .' The time when the text appeared seems to have little in common with our time – except, of course, for the most obvious and general thing: that it was a time of profound social tectonic shifts and turbulence. Despite its generality, this similarity may not be insignificant or merely superficial, especially when we consider the ways in which we – both as individuals and as a society

– are responding to these tectonic shifts, turbulences, and the confusions that accompany them. On the contrary, one might say that disavowal has only now reached the status of 'ordinary perversion' (I borrow the term from Catheryn Barrena Phipps).

Perversion, or more precisely fetishism, was of course already central to Freud's treatment of disavowal. However, one of the important and valuable dimensions of Mannoni's text lies precisely in the fact that he has considerably expanded the concept of disavowal. He has expanded it and linked it to the general structure of *belief* (which he explicitly distinguishes from faith), which comes into play in a whole range of social phenomena and their constitutive illusions. The Austrian philosopher Robert Pfaller, for example, has often referred to Mannoni's work in his writings, emphasizing especially the positive aspects of disavowal-as-belief and its associated 'illusions' (for example, the theatrical illusion, about which Mannoni has also written); he showed in what sense belief and illusions are an indispensable and constitutive dimension of all sociality.[1] This aspect of Mannoni's text is largely left out here, which is not to say that we do not pursue his expansion of the notion of disavowal along a different path – namely the path that expands disavowal to include its neurotic dimension and thus considers it also outside the realm of perversion. This extension is particularly important because only against its background do we get a sense of the significant change that the social structure of disavowal has recently undergone.

Belief Starts with Knowledge

Mannoni gives a series of examples in his text, through which he deploys the plethora of different forms in which disavowal takes place. The *fetishist* disavowal emerges as its most accomplished form, if we might say; and, when he comes to it, Mannoni abruptly concludes his text, as if it was already somehow outside the realm of the question he is dealing with. The fundamental trick of the fetishist disavowal is that it transfers the disavowed belief (the 'but all the same' part) to an object – fetish – liberating the subject from all forms of unconscious belief. This means that it is not even that I unconsciously keep believing what I *know* to be otherwise; in

24

a way, I am free from every belief, even unconscious ones, because it is my fetish that believes
for me. Whereas the phrase 'I know well, but all
the same' is the trade mark or the signature of
disavowal, a fetishist will never say 'but all the
same', since 'his "but all the same" is his fetish.'[2]
As is the case with many other operations associated with the clinical structure of perversion (to
which we will dedicate more time than Mannoni
does), the operation of disavowal is in this case
entirely 'successful'. It leaves no other trace but
the fetish, and, as Freud has already pointed out,
fetishists are perfectly happy with this solution;
they do not usually enter analysis because of their
fetish and the problems it causes them. This is
why perversion often comes across as resistant to
analysis, unreceptive to it: what may appear to
others as a problem is not experienced as a problem or a difficulty: 'For though no doubt a fetish
is recognized by its adherents as an abnormality,
it is seldom felt by them as the symptom of an
ailment accompanied by suffering. Usually they
are quite satisfied with it, or even praise the way
in which it eases their erotic life.'[3]

In other words, no conflict persists here; the
tension is resolved. It is a different story with

neurotics: as Mannoni puts it, they spend their life saying 'but all the same'. Not in a direct way, not by declaring that, after all, they still believe what they know not to be the case, but stating this in many other ways, which constitutes the core of neurotic behaviour. Here, in short, we are in the realm of symptoms and of the possible encumbrances and suffering related to them. The disavowed belief is not entirely externalized and objectified but demands continuous work (of the unconscious), translation, and relocation, and hence persists as a possible source of internal and external conflict.

The most famous example discussed by Mannoni does not involve a fetish but nevertheless exposes perfectly the constitution of 'magical belief' that lies at the core of disavowal. It is an example he takes from the autobiography of the Hopi Indian chief Don Talayesva,[4] translated and published in France in 1959 under the title *Soleil Hopi*, with a preface by Claude Lévi-Strauss. The magical belief at stake in this case is the belief in Katcinas – spirits or gods. At a certain season of the year, the Katcinas appear in the pueblos, much as Santa Claus appears in our culture; and, again like Santa, they take a strong interest in children. They also resemble Santa Claus in that they conspire with parents to deceive the children. The imposture is very strictly maintained, and no one would dare to expose it. Talayesva presents us with the account of how – when presented with the fact that the dancers that children were told were Katcinas are in truth their fathers and uncles wearing masks – at that point he started to believe in the magical presence of Katcinas. The first step is what can be justly described as a traumatizing blow: 'When the Katcinas entered the kiva without masks', Talayesva writes, 'I had a great surprise. They were not spirits. . . . I recognized all of them, and I felt very unhappy, because I had been told all my life that Katcinas were gods. I was especially shocked and angry when I saw that all my clan fathers and uncles were dancing as Katcinas. I felt the worst when I saw my own father.'[5] The next step is that of the disavowal proper, based on the following explanation given by the adults: 'Now you know', the children are told, 'that the *real* Katcinas do not come to dance in the pueblos *the way they did in the old days*. Now they only come invisibly, and, on the days of the dance, they dwell in their masks in mystical fashion.'

At this point (though of course we cannot assume this in all cases, and a sequel may unfold differently) a belief is formed in the *mystical presence* of Katcinas – that is to say, in the real existence of spirits – in spite of the fact that the children now *know very well* that the dancing figures they saw were not Katcinas and that they have never actually seen one. This belief is further facilitated and consolidated by the existing social institutions. We can see here how social institutions and rituals can play a role similar to that of fetish: they take upon themselves the existence of the disavowed belief; they help both to generate and to sustain it.

But the Hopi case also illustrates something else. It shows how (external) institutions can help us appease some traumatic experience (the young Hopi finding out that Katcinas didn't exist) as well as the possible internal conflicts resulting from it. It also shows how this traumatic experience functions in fact as the *condition of our belief* in (social) institutions. If children had not been deliberately misled and systematically encouraged to believe that the Katcinas existed and danced in pueblos, they would also have been spared the traumatic disappointment of discovering that the

Katcinas were in fact their fathers and uncles. In other words, in this case we can see that, socially speaking, traumatic experiences are often deliberately induced (in a controlled environment) in order to make institutions and belief in them work. Rituals of 'initiation' are usually just that: almost never without a certain traumatic dimension, such rituals aim to reinforce institutions that they seemingly undermine by their extra-normativity.[6]

Moreover, and as Mannoni also convincingly shows, it would be a mistake to regard belief as a first, 'childlike' phase of one's relation to the world that is later replaced by enlightened knowledge and to conclude that, because this knowledge is sometimes unpleasant or downright traumatic, *we regress* back into belief or continue to believe what we believed before the better knowledge came along. Belief does not exist before knowledge and its possibly traumatic aspect, but the latter is a condition for the establishment of belief, and belief comes after or at the same time as knowledge. In this respect, too, the case of Talayesva is instructive. It would be a mistake to say that before their initiation the Hopi children naïvely *believed* in the spirits of Katcinas. No, they were objectively deceived. *They didn't know any better* – the phrase is very appropriate here. They believed what they could see, what they could hear, and what they were told by knowing adults (that is to say, by the authorities). In short, it is not that in their naïve credulity they believed some crazy, unbelievable, fairy-tale story: this story was presented to them (by adults) as plausible and objectively true – a lot of effort was put into it. In fact, they only start to believe in the fairy-tale story *after* knowledge intervenes: from that point on, they start to believe in the *mystical*, invisible presence of spirits. The case thus nicely reminds us that belief is strictly correlative to knowledge and is established along with it, even if at a distance from it. As a form of disavowal, this belief requires the disclosure of truth; it *requires knowledge* and its associated blow as its inner condition. This is precisely why – and this is crucial – this belief is *resistant to knowledge*: knowledge cannot be the remedy for disavowal. The emphasis on 'I know well' cannot dissolve the 'but all the same', since 'the sole reason for the "but all the same" is the "I know well".'[7] The knowledge into which the children are initiated at a certain moment, namely that the dancing Katcinas are in fact their fathers and uncles, becomes the basis of belief in the strict sense of the word, belief in the mystical presence of spirits (which dwell in the masks), belief in something that they cannot see directly. Knowledge and belief (as distinct from religious faith) are established simultaneously; they are part of the same experience.

Without undermining Mannoni's conclusions, we might now introduce another or additional emphasis to his. Mannoni connects the trauma, which in the case discussed above lies at the origin of the disavowal, with the blow that the disclosure deals to the children's *conviction that Katcinas exist*. Something that the children thought existed and was real does not in fact exist. The object they thought was an object of their world is actually not. This is of course what connects this situation to the Freudian theory of disavowal as fundamentally disavowal of castration. A brief note on this rather untimely notion is probably in order here. The penis is an organ that occurs only in people who are born biologically male; it can also not be there, which equally threatens those who do have it with the possibility of its being taken away, or of its simply not being there. The non-existence of this organ in the 'other sex' thus accounts for its being con-stitutively, *essentially* marked by the possibility of not being there, with an absence. Hence its Lacanian renaming of it as *phallus* – a concept that includes this dimension of a minus, thus making phallus a universal function, in the sense of something that everybody relates to, regard-less of whether one has 'it' or not. According to Lacan and his reading of Freud, the 'privilege', or the exceptional status, of the phallus comes essentially from this foundational lack or absence rather than from its presence (as an organ). Its appearing against the background of its possi-ble lack or non-being is precisely what accounts for the symbolic rather than simply the anatomic character of the phallus, for its status as a signifier ('a signifier without a signified'). In the seminar *Desire and its Interpretation* Lacan renders this nicely with a quote from *Hamlet*, when Hamlet says: 'The body is with the king, but the king is not with the body. The king is a thing . . . Of nothing.' This then would be the definition of the phallus, in its very non-coincidence with the body or anatomy: 'The body is with the phallus, but the phallus is not with the body. The phallus is a thing . . . of nothing.' And the term 'nothing' must not be taken here just in the derisory sense, as something trifling and insignificant, but also quite literally: phallus is what gives a certain form to the nothing or absence; it is an upholder of nothing. It is the nothing, the minus at its core that gives the phallus its symbolic status and significance.

Now, and to return to our theme, according to Freud, when (usually) a boy first notices the non-existence of the penis in the other sex, he can either recognize the universalizing dimension of castration or else disavow what he saw by making something surrounding this perception of the lack (a shoe, a stocking, underwear . . .) his fetish. In which case this object is endowed with special value, for it makes it possible for us to 'know' that to have a penis is contingent and that it may very well not be there, yet to persist at the same time in the belief that this is not the case. The (sexual) fetish is the object that sustains this belief for us.

In Mannoni's reading of the Talayesva example, this template of fetishist disavowal makes him zoom in on the disclosure of the non-existence of an *object* (the Katcinas) which up to that point was held to exist and to be part of the world. While Mannoni thus mostly remains with this aspect of the traumatic blow, we could add here yet another traumatic dimension of the disclosure, which might be every bit as significant.

For the children not only learn that the dancing Katcinas are not real or not really there but are in fact just their fathers and uncles in disguise; they also learn that they have been *deliberately and systematically deceived by* those very fathers and uncles (with the full cooperation of their mothers). So we are dealing not just with the blow linked to what this new knowledge implies for the reality of Kancinas, namely their possible non-existence, but also with the disclosure that the Other – parents as the locus of knowledge and authority – can be deceitful and untrustworthy. And if we focus now on this other disappointment or 'blow', we soon notice that it has itself two sides and implies two different, albeit interconnected, vectors. One draws *a limit* to the powers of what Lacan calls the big Other, the powers or the authority of the adults: fathers, mothers, uncles and their infallibility. It also – through the initiation by which the children themselves become this Other and cross over to the place from which they themselves will henceforth participate in the deceiving of children – a limit to their own subjective powers and infallibility. Let us call this side of the experience the experience of 'symbolic castration'. The latter already involves the phallus as a symbolic token of exchange rather than an organ: we give up something in order to gain access to the symbolic status and social position. In a different manner from castration anxiety as related to the penis as an organ, symbolic castration is actually a solution to a deadlock: it is a loss through which we also gain. The second vector radically shatters, and at the same time restores – or not – the *trust* on a different basis. After all, and as Mannoni already points out, what can one believe, and who can one trust, if authority is deception? Something other than just the knowledge and the questions related to the existence or non-existence of Katcinas is at stake here. Let us recall Talayesva's words: 'I was especially shocked and angry when I saw that all my clan fathers and uncles were dancing as Katcinas. I felt the worst when I saw my own father.'

We can see that, in this latter case, 'knowledge' has relatively little to do with knowing in the sense of episteme or with the content of that knowing. It implies something else, or more. It is not only the knowledge of the (non-)reality of

Katcinas but just as much the knowledge of the deception/betrayal and of imperfection, unreliability, constituting a limit of the Other, which is revealed on this occasion. In other words, there is nothing neutral, indifferent about this 'blow', nothing reducible to knowing and accepting the facts. We might also say that this other blow bears not on this or that object of the world but, rather, on the conditions of the objectively true knowledge as such. What can one know, if the authority behind objective knowledge is deception? The split between knowledge and belief is not the only split that occurs here; there is also a split inherent to knowledge itself, the split between its content and that which guarantees the truth (objective validity) of this content. The latter – because of its relation to trust and possibly love – is prone to carrying a particularly affective, potentially traumatic dimension.

In the context of the question of the potentially traumatic dimension of knowledge, there comes to mind the famous quote from Freud in which he lists the *blows* that science has dealt to humanity (Copernicus, Darwin and – Freud).[8] One might legitimately ask why, after all, would a new, different knowledge constitute a *blow*, something that hurts and traumatizes us? Obviously not because of its immediate content, but because of its implications and wider meaning. Knowledge in this sense is never just (factual) knowledge, even though it is often presented as such. Freud's emphasis is on the blow that science deals to our narcissism and 'naïve self-love', which puts the accent on the vector we have associated above with the limitation of our powers. In principle, however, the traumatic dimension of this blow could also be linked to learning, if not about a *deliberate* deception (by authorities), at least about how they are or can be deceiving, and hence point to the fact that not even what we hold as 'objective knowledge' is always reliable. This other knowledge (of deception) shatters our trust not only in the authorities but also in the reliability of objective knowledge as such.

Science or Authority?

A short digression into the question of science and authority is in order at this point. The authority of modern science is based – in Karl Popper's terms – on the inherent possibility of falsification – that is, on the falsifiability of all its theories. If a claim or theory cannot be falsified, if it is not inherently testable, it is not scientific.

The credibility of modern science is based on very different principles than (traditional) Authority. However, it is also indisputable that, in its *social functioning*, science has achieved at some point the status of Authority. Which is to say that, although most of us have no means of verifying (or falsifying) scientific discoveries and theories, we take them to be true ('blindly believe' in them) because they are socially recognized and labelled as 'scientific'. To accept something as true because science says it is so is different from the way in which science itself works, which is by relying on the principle of doubt and falsification rather than on any outside Authority. This difference is often blurred in contemporary social media debates, in which refusal to accept the *social authority* of science is justified by invoking the method of its scientific authority, the principle of falsification. So we hear things such as: 'We refuse to blindly believe (trust the social authority of science) and pledge our right to exercise doubt, which is precisely the most scientific thing to do. Is science not supposed to be all about doubt and not taking anything at its face value? We are indeed the true embodiment of the scientific spirit, contrary to the (corrupted) scientists, who just blindly repeat what the Power (politics, capital) wants them to say.' In this way science becomes the justification for not trusting science. This is a very typical confusion of the social authority of science and its scientific authority.

While scientific authority (authority as scientific) is based on doubt, possible falsification, and constant interrogation, the social authority of science is a different matter; it is much more akin to traditional authority in the sense of something that hinges on our (blind) belief and trust. Of course, part of this trust comes from our knowledge about how science operates, about its method being precisely other than that of relying on any outside authority. (We trust science because it doesn't trust anything.) But this doesn't make our belief/trust in science any less about trust and belief. And this is not simply because not all of us are scientists (and we cannot ourselves make the appropriate scientific calculations), for scientists themselves depend and rely on the social authority of science in many ways (including, of course, for the financing of their research).

The recent collapsing of the social authority of science can thus not be attributed simply to a rise of (obscurantist) beliefs, since this social authority itself is based on something like an 'obscurantist' belief (we trust science because it is science). The gap that cannot be directly filled in by any positive knowledge, and thus requires a 'leap of faith', seems irreducible, indispensable for our social and symbolic functioning. Society – and, indeed, science itself as part of society – cannot function as a purely scientific community. This is not the place to engage in a complex debate about the reasons for the collapse of the social authority of science, so let us simply make two related points.

First: it would be erroneous to see in this collapse a sort of *regression* into some pre-modern, pre-scientific modes of knowledge and belief, for the collapse concerns primarily the always contemporary existence of the gap that necessitates blind belief (trust) in scientific claims. Simply put: more and more people refuse to make the 'leap of faith' when it comes to science. A crumbling of the social authority of science, a reluctance or straight-out refusal to trust it, is the cause of undermining (relativizing) its inherently scientific claims and scientific authority, and not the other way around.

Second: if we listen to what these sceptics are saying, how they formulate the reasons for their mistrust, two key words that keep re-emerging are *money* (profit, capital, financial interests) and *surveillance* (monitoring and directing our lives, for monetary or disciplinary purposes). If we momentarily put in parentheses the often extremely picturesque and phantasmatic ways in which these two words orchestrate the narratives of different conspiracy theories, it is only fair to say that what they evoke is not just a product of imagination but part and parcel of our social order. That is to say, and to put it as simply as possible, that science is losing its social authority on account of its being an inherent and important part of the capitalist world order and its dynamics. And increasingly so, since, for example, money for research mostly comes not from the state (as representing public interest) but, rather, from private corporations pursuing private interests. Yes, the answer is boring and predictable: capitalism. It is precisely this capitalist dynamic that fuels (and often justifies) the mistrust in science, its disappearance as social authority. But this causality is not without an interesting twist.

To take just one concrete example of how involvement in capitalist dynamics facilitates the denial of scientifically established facts. It is obviously true that the so-called green transition can bring huge profits to certain corporations, which in turn can actively direct and influence what is socially perceived as green. A very passionate debate, which includes scientists, that has been taking place lately is for example that between the advocates of renewable energy and advocates of nuclear energy. Is it just renewable energy that should count as 'green energy', or also nuclear energy, which leaves a much smaller carbon footprint? In whose interest is it to promote solely renewable energy, even at the price of intensifying the carbon footprint in the process, and in whose interest to promote nuclear energy as the only true alternative? There is clearly 'money and power' behind both options. And there is no way out of this possible suspicion within the existing economic order. Which is why this 'no way out' often results in the conclusion that *there is no climate change*, since it's all just about financial interests. We should recognize this claim for what it is: not simply an obscurantist regression but a disavowal of the traumatic reality of capitalism. Financial interests, which are obviously part of capitalism, are acknowledged and used in a way that shields capitalism's very brutal reality, and the suspicion moves to science. The acknowledgement of the interests of capital serves to divert us from any consequences of this claim, which would be in the direction of concluding that this is therefore not a good economic system. Instead, the consequence (the conclusion) becomes the non-existence of climate change. The perverse syllogism goes as follows: everything in our social life is about money and financial interests, therefore there is no climate change. Something similar happened in the case of Covid. More often than not, a refusal to accept scientific facts, their *denial*, is just one of the forms taken by the disavowal of the truly traumatic dimension of capitalism. The traumatism at stake is not only about social disintegration and environmental disaster related to capitalism but at least as much about what appears as a nightmarish *no way out* of it. In this precise sense, the denial of climate change is a denunciation of capitalism *by proxy*, in much the same way that fetishist disavowal is not a direct denial but a denial by proxy, denial delegated to the fetish. And pointing out financial interests and people who profit from different things is the *means* of this disavowal, because it (re)directs our attention to subjective reasons (greed, enjoyment) and diverts us from the far more traumatic possibility of a greedy and self-enjoying a-subjective system of which no one is really or fully in control. A very interesting link between denial and disavowal appears here. Denial of climate change is in this sense a *result* of the disavowal of the brutal reality of capitalism. And so is the denial of, or refusal to accept, many other scientific facts.

Related to the issue of science losing its social authority is another aspect of capitalism that is more interesting and complex than might seem at first glance. Money has long since taken the throne of social authority, and this is not meant in any moralist sense. Money did not replace symbolic authority; money *is* a symbolic authority in the sense that it is more than itself, it is bigger than itself, it contains a *je ne sais quoi* that – paradoxically – no money can buy. Noam Yuran develops wonderfully in his new book[9] the point that capitalist money, which differs from the way in which money functions in other economies, is not just a means of exchange but also has a use value; it has not only a quantity but a quality. This is why, for example, expensiveness is one of the qualities of luxury products rather than just a description of their price. When rich people buy expensive, even ridiculously expensive things, it is not simply because they can afford them, but because by doing so they buy more than the thing itself; they buy precisely what money (as means of exchange) cannot buy directly – a certain quality. They pay not simply for the expensive thing but for this thing to be expensive, incommensurable (with other ordinary things). They pay so that they can pay (a lot). Still following Yuran: there is also something, a quality, that the rich acquire by *having* their money – that is, by being rich – rather than by giving it away in exchange. I believe this is precisely what Lacan had in mind when, commenting on Adam Smith's *Wealth of Nations*, he made the following laconic remark: 'It is extraordinary that ever since there have been economists, nobody . . . ever made this remark that wealth is the property of the wealthy.'[10] *Wealth is the property (quality) of the wealthy*: one could hardly put it more concisely. Wealth does not simply refer to a certain quantity of money but is an additional something that cannot be quantified: it is a property. The wealthy don't just have a lot of wealth; wealth is also a quality of their being wealthy, something in the wealthy more than their money, or something in money more than money. And it is precisely this circularity, this tautological *gap*, that accounts for the social authority of money, or for money *as authority*. Authority as authority is precisely and always about such a self-referential gap and a surplus. And when we hear – as we often do nowadays – the claim that people today 'have no respect for authority', we should think twice before agreeing with it. For the social respect for money is indisputable, and the authority of money functions very much like any other authority: it is founded on something other than reasonable explanation or quantification.

However, while to have money, to be wealthy, is regarded as a positive quality, or at least as something to be respected, doing things for money is much less noble and still carries the inglorious stamp of prostitution (as Yuran also shows very nicely). It quickly smells of obscenity and corruption. The rich are rich. They may be eccentric, ruthless, brutal, degenerate, but there is one thing they cannot be accused of – namely of doing things for money. Which may seem counter-intuitive, for, clearly, they only employ their forces to get more money, yet the remark stands: people working for them can easily be accused of doing things for money, but the rich themselves somehow don't seem to be 'all about money'. HBO's series *Succession* is a very good demonstration of this aspect of the wealthy. Up to the final twist, which in a sense retroactively dispels the myth that something more than money, something exterior to the less glamorous space and logic of exchange and of doing things for money, is the origin of wealth and represents its essence. Capitalism needs and perpetuates this myth, even if, and when, it gladly and openly 'admits' that the game is all about money. This, again, is a textbook form of disavowal. The wealthy say and gladly admit that it is all about money, but they don't really believe it (they believe that their being, as being of the rich, is not all about money, and that they are somehow special). In fact, it is all about money; but this 'all' involves a spectral dimension, a ghost of authority that must at all costs be prevented from being traced back to money, because this would make it collapse as authority.

Psychoanalysis and Science

Let's return to the two aspects of the blow that knowledge can inflict upon us and dwell a bit more on the one related to the revelation of deception, and hence to the issue of trust. We can see (also in the Hopi example discussed by Mannoni) how, following the disclosure of deception, there is a clear moment of *oscillation and risk* that takes place in relation to trust – a moment of crisis or a critical moment of encountering some disturbing reality. From here on, the question is: will trust be restored on some other basis (which includes among other things, but not necessarily, a disavowed belief), will it reinforce the given social bond and belief, will it induce a new kind of social bond, or will it, rather, remain a continual source of doubt, interrogation, curiosity, distrust, paranoia even?

Let us recall that the philosopher most closely associated with the advent of modern science, namely Descartes, began his seminal work, *Meditations on First Philosophy*, with the assumption of an omnipotent Deceiver, an 'evil genius', an Other constantly deceiving us about everything.

> I will therefore suppose that, not God, who is perfectly good and the source of truth, but some evil spirit, supremely powerful and cunning, has devoted all his efforts to deceiving me. ... But whenever this preconceived opinion of God's supreme power occurs to me, I cannot help admitting, that, if indeed he wishes to, he can easily bring it about that I should be mistaken, even about matters that I think I intuit with the eye of the mind as evidently as possible.[11]

Modern science and its philosophical foundation of certainty, on the one hand, and the idea of the possibility of a deceptive, deceitful big Other (of Authority), not so different from the adults of the Hopi example, on the other, coincide in this Cartesian figure. This is certainly significant. It is this very presupposition of a deceiving spirit that clears the ground for the scientific method and for the establishment of a knowledge that would break with the reliance on any external Authority and find the point of certainty elsewhere (although Descartes re-establishes the trust in Authority/God in the next step of his argument).

And we might ask what, after all, is scientific knowledge in its modern, mathematized and universally transmittable form? It is not knowledge about deception and castration/limitation but knowledge of a certain factual content that puts the other two (affective) dimensions of knowledge in parentheses.

And it is here that it becomes clear in what way psychoanalysis is nevertheless different from science, or how Freud is different from Copernicus and Darwin: not in that psychoanalysis emphasizes things other than knowledge but in that it is concerned above all with that *knowledge* which science both produces and cuts off, exempting it from its further calculations and advances. It is, in short, about what we might call *collateral knowledge* and its potentially traumatic dimension. This is what lies at the heart of Lacan's insistence that the Freudian unconscious is not some romantic dimension of subjectivity that escapes or is heterogeneous to knowledge, but that it is precisely about knowledge. The unconscious is a form of knowledge, a 'knowledge that does not know itself.' Two further Lacanian claims are related to this: 'the unconscious *thinks*' (and is never simply irrational), and 'the subject of the unconscious is the Cartesian subject.' These two and similar Lacanian claims have often been criticized for rendering psychoanalysis too cerebral, too intellectual, at the expense of the affective dimension. But these claims, on the contrary, derive precisely from the discovery of the affective (potentially traumatic) dimension of knowledge itself, the inseparability of the two dimensions. In this respect, the only thing of which Lacan is guilty is not succumbing to a dualistic view that would try to separate the two dimensions – body/spirit, emotion/intellect, affect/knowledge – and to emphasize one at the expense of the other.

To recapitulate: the result of disavowal is that knowledge remains in play; one can talk about it calmly and not deny its content, but the reality (of this knowledge) is lost. The subject can access this knowledge (as opposed to repressed knowledge), but it *doesn't mean* for her what it normally means. And this would be another way of putting it: in disavowal, a certain knowledge acquires a different meaning or is deprived of its meaning (in terms of implications). If we formulate Talayesva's reasoning on this basis, we might say the following: '(I know that) Katcinas don't really dance in pueblos, but *that doesn't mean* that they aren't there.' Or: '(I know that) Katcinas don't really dance in pueblos, but *that doesn't mean* that the adults simply misled and lied to me when they claimed that they did.'

We will return to some of these questions in more detail further on, but we can already anticipate the following. What comes to the fore in contemporary forms of both disavowal and denial is the absolute emphasis on deceit (rather than on the *reality* involved in this deceit). The really important thing is no longer whether Katcinas exist or not, but the fact that we are possibly being deceived about it. This shift of emphasis can take the form of the obsession with the Other constantly deceiving and manipulating us, as in the case of conspiracy theories; it can take the form of a 'post-factual' worldview in which the content of knowledge becomes relativized, while *our relation* to that content itself obtains the status of an object and is considered as 'objective' as anything else (even if it is 'false', it is a fact to be reckoned with); it can also take the form of our most common everyday fear of being somebody's dupe, of being perceived as naïve, of not being in the loop – and hence lacking in 'social capital'. In other words, disavowal doesn't need to take the drastic form of a conspiracy theory. It can take a much more 'reasonable', moderate, but also more perverse form of what Nietzsche called 'the lulling opium of skepticism'.[12] *We know better* than to allow anything to really get to us.

As superficial as these phenomena may seem, they form part of profound tectonic shifts that also have a significant philosophical background that can help us understand the logic associated with some of these recent 'twists and turns'.

Cogito: An Escape to Being?

We have already introduced Descartes: his hypothesis of an omnipotent Deceiver and its role in establishing certainty. If we put Cartesian procedure alongside the classical mechanism of disavowal, we can see in what way Descartes differs and is more radical than the latter. Perhaps the simplest way to describe the difference between them would be this: in Descartes we are dealing not with a split within knowledge but with a split between knowledge and being. However, and as we shall see, the two are not unrelated.

At the heart of the Cartesian procedure is the point at which methodical, hyperbolic doubt in everything I know produces certainty of (my) being. Part of methodical doubt is the hypothesis of an evil genius, a deceiving God, who can lead me astray about absolutely everything, including the most obvious rational truths. (We have already seen: 'But whenever this preconceived opinion of God's supreme power occurs to me, I cannot help admitting that, if indeed he wishes to, he can easily bring it about that I should be mistaken, even about matters that I think I intuit with the eye of the mind as evidently as possible.') Following the path of methodical doubt, Descartes concludes that I can in fact doubt absolutely everything I know, even the things that I hold to be most obviously true, and that I must indeed doubt everything I know. At this precise and vertiginous point, at which the certainty of what I *know* disappears completely, another kind of certainty appears, the certainty of being: . . . *therefore I am*. '*Dubito ergo cogito, cogito ergo sum*', can be translated as 'I doubt; therefore I think, therefore I am.' Or, put another way: even if absolutely everything I know is false, a result of deception and illusion, I am still the subject of this (false) knowledge; I have these (false) thoughts, therefore I am.

Let's stop there for a moment. For we can legitimately question the continuity that is supposed to guide this process, the continuity that Descartes locates in knowledge. When doubt seizes all knowledge of things, of rational ideas, and of ourselves, we are left with knowledge of only one certain thing: the knowledge of our being. But is this really knowledge? Is this certainty knowledge? Are they of the same texture? Are certainty and knowledge one and the same thing? Are thinking and knowing that I think one and the same thing? Is certainty the last (and only) knowledge that remains, or are we dealing with a discontinuity and a gap?

Indeed, it could be argued that Cartesian methodological doubt produces not only and simply the certainty of being but a *split between knowing and being*, so that at the extreme point of the *cogito* argument we also get a glimpse of their mutual exclusion. The price of certainty is the discontinuity between one and the other, between knowing and being. Methodological doubt gradually and inexorably corners us, places us in a position where we either 'are' or 'know'. There is no direct continuity between the two; when I know that I am, I am no longer in the certainty of being but already in its after-effect.

Moreover, and to enhance this point a little further, one might ask: is '*cogito ergo sum*' the ultimate *proof of* my being, or is it rather something like an *escape* into being (from the plethora of different, dubious thoughts)? Descartes sets up his argument so that it points to a substance or being that *has* all these thoughts (even if they are false). He is therefore suggesting a pre-existence of substance or being. But what if this substance, this something that appears as pure being, becomes 'pure being' or substance only in the gesture of *ejecting itself* out of these thoughts with which it is entangled, hence splitting with all knowledge, or with knowledge as such? Can the Cartesian procedure not be described as a procedure in which I, so to speak, *doubt myself out* of all knowledge as possibly deceptive, in order to be? We can add a further question to this: does this mean that *cogito* is an escape from madness, as some have developed, for example Michel Foucault,[13] or does it rather mean that *cogito* is the inaugural point of madness, in the sense that it coincides in its structure with the inaugural point of the unconscious, its constitution? In which case it would be possible to argue that *cogito is* the unconscious.

Lacan came to read the *cogito* in this second way, particularly in his Seminar XIV (*The Logic of Fantasy*, 1966–7),[14] which reverses his previous reading from Seminar XI (*The Four Fundamental Concepts of Psychoanalysis*) in which *cogito* appears as the obverse side of the unconscious. This shift is most interesting, so let us take a closer look at it. What remains the same in both readings is the claim that the structure of the *cogito* argument is the structure that Lacan calls 'alienation' – that is to say, the structure of an *either–or*: I either think or I am; I cannot have both, for their intersection is empty or impossible. *Cogito* as proof of being cannot be firmly established beyond the fleeting moment of its utterance; it is true only at the moment when I say it. All certainty is in fact localized solely in the point of my saying 'I think', 'I am'.[15] Beyond that I already have to rely on something else, namely on the Other as guarantor of the continuity between these two moments of knowledge and as guarantor of meaning, including the meaning in which I can be said to exist. And this in turn exposes the fact that the structure at stake here is indeed that of alienation, which has the further specificity that its either–or does not in fact really allow us to choose one or the other but implies a *forced choice* (illustrated by Lacan with the famous example 'Your money or your life'; if I choose money, I lose both, so I can only choose life, and have life without money). So not only is the intersection of being and thinking empty (except for the fleeting moment of saying *cogito*), I also have no option other than to choose thinking, which Lacan identifies here (in Seminar XI) with meaning. I can only choose meaning (the existence in the Other as the locus of signifiers), but with this choice I lose the immediate certainty of my being: my being is now mediated by the Other; the Other is the locus, the symbolic structure that precedes me and determines that, and what, I am. Another way of putting this would be to say that I only exist in the Other, in and through the 'symbolic'.

We should further note that this reading also resonates with Descartes' solution of the problem of which he is well aware: how to break out of

the limited confines of my being as the only certain knowledge, how to bridge the gap between
the knowledge of my being (the 'knowing' that
I am) and the true knowledge of *what* I am, and
what everything else is. In Descartes this gap can
only be bridged by (re)introducing an instance
of a non-deceitful, infinite, and omniscient God
who guarantees the correctness of my knowing
even when I cannot derive it from a zero point of
certainty or think about it constantly. As is well
known, Descartes has recourse at this point to
the ontological proof of the existence of (a non-
deceiving) God. In the simplest terms, we might
say that *trust* in the Other becomes the condition
of my *knowledge*.

In order to establish a science (true knowledge)
of the external world, as well as of ourselves as *res
extensae* – i.e., as bearers of sensible qualities – it
is necessary to assume/prove the existence of a
God who is not deceitful, who created eternal
truths, and, as Descartes puts it, planted them
in our souls as seeds. This God is not a religious
God but the God of philosophers and scientists
(following Pascal's distinction between 'the God
of Abraham, Isaac, and Jacob' and 'the God of
philosophers and scientists'). Man thus becomes

the subject of knowledge and dominates the world, but only as the depository of the truths of the Other.[16] The philosophical debate continued with empiricism, which questioned Descartes' rationalist gesture and culminated in Hume contesting the validity of the very notion of causality, which in turn woke Kant from his 'dogmatic slumber' and led to a theory of the transcendental that excluded from the realm of knowledge the knowledge of things as they are *in themselves*. The story is well known, as is its aftermath, all the way to Quentin Meillassoux and his significant reinterrogation of this development in *After Finitude*.

However, and returning to the core of the *cogito* argument, we might say that all this development was made possible by the conversion (already at work in Descartes) of mutual exclusion, the split between being and knowledge into the split *within* knowledge, a split inherent to knowledge. And it would seem that psychoanalysis follows the same train of thought, with its concept of unconscious knowledge as 'knowledge that doesn't know itself'.

If we read Lacan's seminar on the *Logic of Fantasy*, we get a somewhat different and, I would say, much more interesting picture. In this seminar Lacan cuts straight to the innards of modern philosophy with a bold speculative claim: the split within knowledge is already a *consequence*, a repercussion of the split between being and knowing implicit in the *cogito*. Lacan now claims that, if we look more closely at the *cogito* argument, we see that the split or disjunction of thinking and being never really disappears, *not even at the moment of uttering ego cogito, ego sum*. Instead, Lacan now sees this split as the very ground of the constitution of the unconscious. How?

We are returning to a point made earlier: certainty (of being) is not the same thing as knowledge. And this, I would argue, is precisely what is at the core of Lacan's new reading of the *cogito*. Reduced to its gist, this new reading is actually quite simple. Lacan reverses the previous perspective and claims that what comes to the fore with the Cartesian *cogito* is in fact the choice of *being* as a forced choice – a forced choice, that is, which can take place only at the expense of thinking (whereas before the forced choice was that of meaning/thinking). As a matter of fact, Lacan now reads Descartes more literally and, rather than spinning the latter's initial argument around, as he does in his first reading, reiterates it, albeit in much stronger terms. By 'stronger terms' I am referring to how he now describes Descartes' procedure of evacuating all possible, and possibly deceitful, knowledge in the process of establishing certainty, as '*throwing thought in the waste bin*'.[17] We might also call it thinking the thought(s) away, thinking oneself out of thinking anything. Descartes treats the *cogito*, or thinking, as 'garbage', as 'junk'; he throws it away in order to establish the certainty of being, or, simply, in order to establish being. As suggested earlier, another way of putting this would be to say that this something that appears as pure being, or being qua being, becomes being or substance only in the gesture of *ejecting itself* out of the thoughts with which it is entangled, and splitting with all knowledge, or with knowledge as such. Certainty of being is a moment at which thoughts remain outside, so to speak.

The result of this new perspective suggested by Lacan is that *cogito* (thinking) now appears no longer as the opposite or the other side of the unconscious but *as the unconscious*. Cartesian *cogito* describes the logical moment of the constitution of the unconscious. Thinking that is cut off and goes into the waste bin is precisely the unconscious.

The constitution of the unconscious coincides not with *repressing* this or that but with something falling out or being excluded, thrown away. The difference is important, because we are not here on the level of psychology but on the level of (ontological) constitution, on the level of being as established with certainty through an act that cuts, disentangles it from thought(s) with which it appears. Being qua being is being amputated of thoughts with which it emerges. However – and this will be Lacan's crucial addition – this thing that is not there, this 'cut off part', does not disappear without leaving a trace, a gap: and this *gap* is the unconscious properly speaking, the consistency of the unconscious is that of a gap. The unconscious is a gap in being, and this gap in being has a certain positive, albeit 'spectral' consistency: it is, so to speak, a non-being that is. It *ex-sists*.

It is important to acknowledge two things here. First, psychology is secondary in this disjunction between being and thinking. I can repress this or that thought (or refuse to see it as my thought) because it conflicts with my psychological anchoring, but what we are discussing here is more fundamental: it is a split constitutive of subjectivity, not a split induced *by* our subjectivity. Second, and even more importantly, it is not simply that, from time to time, unconscious thoughts force their entry from this other space, which in this case would be something like a container of (all) unconscious thoughts. No, the unconscious is primarily a *thinking process*, and not a container. It is something in itself temporal and labouring, rather than just sitting there. 'The unconscious thinks' – which is how Lacan renders the gist of Freud's discovery – means exactly that. It is not stuck in some other place; it is an activity.

And this unconscious, where (often surprising) thinking occurs, is where I'm not. 'The unconscious is the place where I'm not.'[18] Which is why *not-me*, as in 'this is not me', 'I didn't say/mean this', constitutes the marker of the unconscious. This comes particularly to the fore in the impersonal grammatical structure of fantasy, which articulates my *being* (in terms of *jouissance*) by eliminating me from the picture. Fantasy always takes the form of an objective description or a neutral sentence, as in the famous fantasy discussed by Freud: 'A child is being beaten.'

So, the unconscious is not simply a place or a scene (*der anderer Schauplatz*, 'the Other scene'), it is also a thinking that goes on there and makes unexpected *things happen*. And when things happen – *and they never fail to happen* – I find myself in a repeated yet contrary version of the (inaugural) forced choice, in which I could choose only being – I couldn't choose the unconscious, I couldn't choose the slip of the tongue, for example. What happens now is that, in a way, the *latter chooses me*.[19] What is conveyed by a slip of the tongue or a dream is not some deeper or more reliable truth but, rather, the certainty that *thinking goes on* even though *I am not there* as the subject of this thinking – that is, even if I am not where I think, or if I think where I am not. And, when this happens, a psychoanalytic ear is there to notice it and listen. And it can accompany me to the place where I am not, to the place of thinking.

The certainty of being is not the only possible form of certainty. There is also knowing something with certainty but at the cost of being. And we should notice the inflection here: knowing with certainty is not the same thing as being right or wrong about what I know; certainty is not an epistemic category but, rather, an existential category. Solemn moments that we (and world literature) refer to by phrases such as, 'at that moment, I knew with absolute certainty' are usually moments of the deepest existential anxiety; more often than not they convey a deeply disquieting affect.

Psychoanalysis points to anxiety as a paradoxical form of certainty, and it does not simply repudiate anxiety or try to eliminate (medicate) it as quickly as possible. Unlike some psychological theories which associate anxiety with uncertainty, the Lacanian perspective conceives of anxiety not as a reaction or a defence against (unpleasant) uncertainty but as a form of 'awful certainty', a 'signal' of the real, a feeling 'that does not deceive'; anxiety is the outside of doubt, *le hors de doute*.[20] The certainty at stake here, however, is not the certainty of being but, rather, the certainty of thinking that goes on out there, where I am not, and in this sense the certainty of non-being. One might say that anxiety – which is different from fear – is the closest we can get to the experience of the lack-of-being without repression or disavowal. Anxiety-as-certainty could be called an *affect* of the lack-of-being. This is why anxiety plays an important role in psychoanalysis: it can be used to orient us in analysis, and it needs to be administered in the right dosages, as Lacan puts it. In short, we need to work with it, through it. We have to work with it, because, as an affect of non-being, it keeps us close to thinking, knowing. And it directs us in the movement of 'traversing the fantasy', which is one of Lacan's formulations describing the end/goal of analysis.

Psychoanalysis does not end in anxiety, and this – usually paralyzing – certainty of non-being is not in any way its final step. Rather, the end of analysis implies something like shifting this paralyzing dimension of non-being into a gear, transforming it into a movement, a drive of what *is*. It allows for the non-being to become what it is and what it always has been, namely the void at the core of being or substance and, *as such*, its subject.

This is how Lacan now reads Freud's famous guideline *Wo Es war, soll Ich werden*: it is not about the *replacement* of the *Es* (of the unconscious and of the drives) with a rational and conscious agency (Ego or I), it is about a movement that brings out

67

their speculative identity. It is important to note that we are not talking about recognition, about 'being able to recognize oneself' in something. For example, to take the case of the child-beating fantasy: the point is not that, at the end of analysis, it turns out that it is I who is beating a child (or 'wants' to beat a child), or that I am the child who is being beaten (or 'wants' to be beaten) – this is not what the analysis of the fantasy arrives at. It is not about what I (secretly, unconsciously) want or think but about *where I am situated* in the structure. I don't have that thought; I *am* that thought. Lacan's point here is precisely that the subject is not the one who thinks or has these thoughts or fantasies, nor is it the object of these fantasies – say the beaten child; rather, the subject is quite literally the 'it' (*ça*) that structures these fantasies, these thoughts. Grammatically speaking, this 'it' as subject is the same as the 'it' that appears in sentences such as 'it rains' or 'it goes without saying'; even when the impersonal 'it' doesn't explicitly appear, it sustains the subjectless structures such as 'a child is being beaten'.

We've come a long way from the starting point of this excursion into Descartes and the *cogito*. So let's recapitulate the points essential to our discussion of disavowal and denial. The hypothesis of a deceiving Other is the method used by Descartes to arrive at one single point of certainty, which later on necessitates the reintroduction of the Other as a matter of a leap of faith. It is this leap of faith and the Other related to it that have been in a situation of profound crisis for some time now. This is not to say that the figure of the big Other has collapsed *as such*; rather, it is being replaced by a figure of the Other as an omnipotent Deceiver and Manipulator, or else as the Other whose principal role is to help us sustain our disavowed beliefs. Psychoanalysis, in the Lacanian version, proposes a different path: trusting the uncertain thoughts to produce the truth – that is, to produce knowledge as truth by their own means. This, then, would be the Lacanian *cogito*, in which the coincidence of being and knowing is not the starting point but the result of a movement; it can only be mediated, arrived at. The starting point of subjectivity is not a repression of this or that thing but the repression of non-being, which returns and manifests itself as a split in knowledge. This split is all we have to work with; we cannot access the non-being directly. The split in knowledge can have many inconvenient aspects, to put it mildly, and comes up with many interesting and baffling 'formations'. But it can also be very convenient, as in the case of disavowal ('I know well, but all the same', which is to say, 'I know, but I don't really know').

As constitutive of subjectivity this repression of non-being, which coincides with the constitution of the unconscious, is not something I can chose not to 'do' – I have no proper choice there: it is a forced choice, yet a choice that I can eventually reiterate, return to, and repeat with a difference that makes a difference. Disavowal, on the other hand, is precisely about refusing to return to that point and clinging instead onto the 'I don't think in order to be (and enjoy).' This of course does not simply mean that I do not think at all, in the sense of not exercising my cognitive abilities – everybody 'thinks' in that sense. What the disavowal is about could, rather, be defined as follows: I exercise my cognitive abilities, and abundantly so, in order not to *think*. I'm smarter than to think. I know better than to think.

Knowledge as Fetish

Let us return from this perspective to the case of Talayesva and to the question of the disavowal of castration as a formal Freudian template of disavowal. We have already specified two different notions of castration, empirical and symbolic. Symbolic castration (which plays a key part in initiation rituals, for example) could also be defined as that which reconfigures the problems of immediate *physical* differences and limitations into a symbolically mediated dialectical issue. It 'elevates' physical powerlessness (helplessness, impotence) into a logical *impossibility* (which, as logical or symbolic, is *manageable*). This is why, from the Lacanian perspective, castration is deeply ambiguous in itself; it functions not simply as a threat and cause of anxiety but also as a solution to a threat.

We can actually see this very clearly if we look at Talayesva's story from a slightly reverse perspective, which can also be drawn from Freud himself, namely the perspective Freud establishes in his *Totem and Taboo*.[21] If we take 'castration' and its operation to be concerned primarily with the question of enjoyment (my enjoyment and the enjoyment of the Other), we cannot pass over the myth that Freud proposes in that essay. He presents us with the image of the primal father (father of the primal horde), which is the image of an all-powerful, insatiable and capricious Other, who is not constrained by any law and who has access to unlimited enjoyment (an exclusive right over all women). The sons unite and kill (and eat) this father, thus establishing a community of brothers as equals, a community in which no one now has the right to 'full' unrestricted enjoyment. In short, all must consent to this 'castration' (limitation of their enjoyment), which functions as the basis of all social formation or community, and which takes place against the background of the mythical (as well as threatening, oppressive) full enjoyment of the Other. Although this uncastrated Other exists only in retroactive fantasy, figurations of this kind of oppressive, sinister enjoyment of an omnipotent and unlimited Other can of course appear in everyday reality and arouse an intense anxiety.

If we go back to Talayesva's story with this in mind, we can actually see how the issue of 'castration' is much more interesting and complicated in this case, too. What is it that actually constitutes the moment of real horror, the climax of the crisis, in his story? It can be placed exactly at the moment when the adults from Talayesva's environment suddenly appear – as what? Not as the 'castrated' (weak, limited) Other but, on the contrary, as the all-powerful, capricious Other, who uses children as toys in its rituals, revels in their gullibility, deliberately deceives them. And this – which is crucial! – *without there being any real Katcinas* to put an end to it, to bind, to 'castrate' the adults, so to speak. Couldn't we say that this momentary appearance, this glimpse – which occurs at the moment of disclosure – at the potentially unlimited enjoyment of the Other, is what paves the way for Talayesva to immediately grab hold of the magic of castration ('Katcinas exist after all; this is not just about my parents and other adults'). He is, quite literally, saved by magic, which in this case does not mean that he is magically saved – saved as if by magic; rather, it means that he is saved by the step into magical belief. He is saved by the constitution of the belief that real Katcinas *do exist after all*, even if they don't really dance in the pueblos. And the adults offer the children this solution, as it were, on a platter, at just the right moment.

So, perhaps paradoxically, we should actually say that the belief in Katcinas in this case does not so much disavow castration as *help to enact and sustain* the symbolic castration of the Other, or of the community as a whole. It says something such as: *and yet* there is something that is 'above' them and that limits their powers. The Other (of) the Other here acts as the support of castration.

The figure of the omnipotent, oppressive Other, at whose mercy we are, gives rise to a moment of intense anxiety. Is this anxiety 'castration anxiety'? Could we simply say that the image of the Other's unlimited enjoyment, the image of the uncastrated Other, is 'castrating' for the subject? Is it, in short, simply a configuration of 'it is either me or you', 'my enjoyment or your enjoyment', that we are dealing with? No, the situation is not symmetrical, because the subject already appears, takes place in the field of the Other, on its ground. The consequence is that the 'castration', the limitation of the Other, cannot take place unless the subject renounces her own enjoyment. The 'castration' (limitation) of the Other happens only if our stake in this game is our own castration/limitation. This is what Freud is saying with the myth from *Totem and Taboo*, and Lacan formalizes it with his concept of alienation. The latter, as we saw, is also not symmetrical: it implies not only an either–or but also a forced choice.

However, and this is Lacan's crucial addition to this symbolic trade or exchange: neurosis (as a most common, ordinary state) is a way in which the subject tries – *secretly, without the Other's noticing/knowing* – to retain some enjoyment, to hide it from the Other – in short, to keep a little of it for himself, outside this exchange. However, it is precisely through this secret malversation (by which the subject presumably steals something from the Other, or from the Other's knowledge) that the subject remains entirely dependent on the instance of the Other. Not only in respect of the (unconscious) guilt but – more surprisingly and paradoxically – in respect of his or her enjoyment: the Other has to sustain the (im)possibility of the subject's enjoyment in order for the subject *to be able to enjoy (at least a little)*. For this little bit of enjoyment is all that the subject can handle without falling prey to anxiety (triggered by the possibility of full, unrestricted enjoyment).

On the other hand, and perhaps contrary to what might be expected, perversion is a subjective structure in which I fully accept castration;[22] I accept it without any hidden remainder. But I do so in a kind of double trade in which I now make the enjoyment of the Other my own – or, rather, in which I make it dependent on my manoeuvres, putting it under my control. All the drama moves to the scene of the Other. I position myself either as the instrument of the Other's enjoyment (as is the case in sadism) or as the object of the Other's enjoyment, which I pre-frame with some agreed, contractual scenario (as in the case of masochism). This poses the question as to whether the full acceptance of castration in perversion 'is, in fact, not the most inaccessible disavowal of castration there could be.'[23] Indeed, herein lies the crucial question of perversion, as well as of the relationship between disavowal and 'castration', which we have seen is by no means simple or straightforward.

The difference between the neurotic modality of 'accepting' castration and its perverse modality might be seen in the fact that, in neurotic modality, some element of repression persists (the Other does not know, cannot/should not know, about my secret bit of enjoyment), while in perverse disavowal everything is actually out in the open; there seem to be no secrets. I can calmly and openly say anything and make the Other blush (but I never blush myself). I know the ins and outs of enjoyment and use this knowledge to provoke the enjoyment of the Other and then make the Other choke on it. I enjoy through the Other, I repress through the Other, but I am the master of ceremonies of this alienation which, *du coup*, ceases to be operative as alienation (implying an either–or, neither–nor, and a forced choice): the impossibility of the intersection is suspended; I can have my cake and eat it, too.

However, we should stress again that not all forms of disavowal, and not even all forms of fetishist disavowal (that is, disavowal involving an actual fetish), have this doubly perverse structure. What is crucial for this structure is not simply the existence of fetishes but a surplus knowledge that orchestrates their deployment vis-à-vis the Other. It is, in a way, a knowledge about functioning of the fetishist disavowal. It is a knowledge that could be formulated like this: 'I know very well that "I know very well, but all the same. . . ."' So we are dealing not only with disavowal but also with configuration in which I use the knowledge itself of its functioning as a fetishist tool. Let me explain this.

To illustrate how a fetish works, Slavoj Žižek tells a story about a man whose wife was diagnosed with acute breast cancer and who died three months later; the husband survived her death unscathed, being able to talk coolly about his traumatic last moments with her – but how? Was he a cold, distant, and unfeeling monster? Soon, his friends noticed that, while talking about his deceased wife, he always held a hamster in his hands, her pet object and now his fetish – the embodied disavowal of her death. When, a couple of months later, the hamster died, the man broke down and had to be hospitalized for a long period. Žižek concludes:

> So, when we are bombarded by claims that in our post-ideological cynical era nobody believes in the proclaimed ideals, when we encounter a person who claims he has been cured of any beliefs, accepting social reality the way it really is, one should always counter such claims with the question: OK, but where is your hamster – the fetish which enables you to (pretend to) accept reality 'the way it is'?[24]

It is at this point that we might situate the (doubly) perverse mode of disavowal, which replies to the above question in effect: Of course I have a hamster, and I *know* how it works, so what's the problem? However, rather than bringing us closer to reality, 'the way it is', this knowledge and its deployment have the effect of sealing off the reality more completely, making it all the more inaccessible. Why? Because in this configuration knowledge itself starts to function as a fetish/object that makes it possible to *disavow the disavowal itself* (of which we are 'well aware'). So we actually end up with two hamsters rather than with the raw reality – reality 'such as it is'.

What we are dealing with is thus a configuration in which *knowledge* about some traumatic reality (the 'I know well') gets strangely redoubled or split and *itself* starts playing the role of the object that protects us against this traumatic reality. 'Knowledge' thus adopts a new and different role; it is no longer simply something to be disavowed but – paradoxically – something that can help us disavow (the real of this same knowledge). As we shall see in the next section, rather than with a disavowal of castration, we are dealing with its possible use value and controlled deployment.

Unlike that raised by classical disavowal, the question is therefore no longer simply why does the knowledge about something, why do revelations such as 'the emperor is naked', not really work, so that we continue to believe and behave as if we didn't know? The question now is, rather, how this kind of knowledge and these kinds of revelations themselves *actively help* to maintain the very illusion they are supposedly destroying.

This is to say that a permutation also occurs at the level of 'but all the same', which presupposes a certain opposition, a contradiction: the structure 'I know well, but nevertheless (or *in spite of it*) I continue to believe the opposite' mutates into 'I know well, and *that's why* I can keep my belief and enjoy this belief undisturbed.' Or: I see it, I acknowledge it, and this is why I can now forget about it.

The fetishization of knowledge thus needs to be taken here in the clinical rather than the metaphorical sense: what is at stake is not that knowledge is highly valued, overemphasized, and in this sense 'fetishized'; what is at stake is that – in a kind of overlapping – knowledge takes the structural place of the fetish as that *via* which we can keep doing, enjoying, or simply ignoring things that this knowledge would seem to contradict. All that is important is that we 'know all about it', and that we are 'nobody's dupes'. This helps us efficiently to de-realize the reality of what is going on, to maintain it as doubly inaccessible. This does not mean, however, that in this structure there can be no moments of crisis.

Casanova: Castration and its Use Value

The other important example that Mannoni analyses in his text describes just such a moment of crisis that appears within a (doubly) perverse structure, and we can use it to make the claims developed above resonate in a more concrete way. This other example is that of Casanova and comes from his work *History of My Life*[25] (also translated as *The Story of My Life*). Without recapitulating the details of the particular episode discussed by Mannoni, let us just recall the basic parameters essential for our reading here. Casanova enormously enjoys playing a magician, provoking and maintaining the credulity, the superstitiousness of Others. The crisis comes when reality accidentally overtakes his abracadabra machinations and a storm breaks in the midst of his magic act, staged for the gaze of a naïve Other, Genoveffa, yet in the accidental absence of this Other. In a moment of panic, Casanova begins to believe that the chalk circle in which he is standing is indeed magical and protects him from being struck by lightning. 'In the terror which overtook me I persuaded myself that if the flashes of lightning I saw did not strike me down it was because they could not enter the circle. But for my false belief . . . I should not have remained in the circle for as long as a minute.'[26]

If we first put Casanova's story alongside Talayesva's, what do we notice? That Casanova's position is in a way similar to that of the adults (the parents) in Talayesva's story – adults who impersonate the spirits of Katcinas for the children (with the sole difference that, in Casanova's story, it is other gullible adults who play the role of the children). What would the moment of crisis in Casanova's story correspond to in Talayesva's story? The answer: if something were to happen during the performance of the Katcinas dance ritual that could present, for the adults themselves, the spirits as real and not just as enacted by them; if an unforeseeable, unexpected event were to take place that could reinforce the reality of the spirits; if, in other words, a surplus realization of the adults' deceptive machinations were to occur, a surplus realization that could surprise the adults themselves. In short: the crisis would occur in this case if the hocus-pocus staged by the adults suddenly became more real than they themselves believed. For that is exactly what happens to Casanova. Because of a chance event (a thunderstorm breaking at just the right moment, combined with the fact that there is no credulous Other on the scene at that moment to be taken in by him), Casanova falls victim to his own magic (in which he cheerfully proclaims his disbelief at all times). For a moment, he thinks that maybe it is all real after all, and thus dares not step outside the circle he now believes protects him from the lightning.

However, in all this, we must not forget that this crisis is also and precisely Casanova's defence. The creepy becoming-real of the magic is the flip side of an (even more frightening) becoming-real, namely the manifestation of an impossible, unbridled, unconstrained enjoyment of the Other at the moment when the storm breaks out – this at least is how Casanova reads the storm: 'I recognized an avenging God who had lain in wait for me there to punish me for all my misdeeds and thus end my unbelief by death.' This manifestation of the enjoyment and the fury of an Other, which he does not control, provokes a crisis. And, when that happens, what is it that Casanova calls to his rescue? Precisely the *magic of castration*. He literally pulls castration out of his hat as a defensive strategy. He himself articulates that quite explicitly when he describes how this event changed his relationship to Genoveffa, the peasant to whom he returns after the event, and who is the credulous Other that he intended to take advantage of with his artifice. These are his words: 'She no longer seemed to be of a different sex from mine, *since I no longer felt that mine was different from hers.* At the moment an idea whose superstitiousness took nothing from its power made me believe that the girl's innocence was protected and that I should be struck dead if I dared to assail it.'

What is actually going on here? Magic belief is what momentarily opens the door of castration. We might describe the situation like this: Casanova gives up his enjoyment in order to appease a vengeful God, literally using castration as an instrument, a tool that he can use in this moment of crisis, or when he needs it, and then forget about it again (as indeed he does) – put it back in the drawer, as it were. Isn't Casanova saying something like 'I don't believe in the (magic of) castration, but I can still resort to it if necessary'? This is a question not so much of disavowing castration as it is of 'appropriating' it. The appropriation removes from it the dimension that is 'beyond our power/control', and which in itself constitutes a crucial element of what is called castration. And of course one might also say that this 'appropriation' is precisely what (perverse) disavowal is actually about, and how it differs from simple repression or, for example, denial. What is disavowed is not simply castration as such but the traumatic dimension (the real) of castration, and it is disavowed precisely by 'inventing' castration as a tool, an instrument. In this precise sense, it might be said that castration is used here as a defence against castration.

The storm that breaks out is the bit of the real that scares Casanova; it brings to light the crack in his 'philosophical system' (as he proudly calls it), the crack that he disavows. Castration, on the other hand, is for him part of the system, part of his philosophical system. His position might be expressed as follows: 'I don't believe in the (magic of) castration, but I still resort to it when necessary.' The permutation or doubling up then also occurs in that the denied belief itself functions as a useful, convenient tool (to be used as needed and to make life easier). We are dealing with something similar in the case of superstition and its denial. Let us recall the famous anecdote of when a journalist visited Niels Bohr and saw that he had a horseshoe (considered as a protective talisman) hanging over his door. 'Is the professor superstitious?', he asked him. 'Of course not', replied the scientist, 'but I'm told that horseshoes bring luck even to those who do not believe in them.' Let us leave aside the question to what extent Bohr's answer is the product of wit. In its literal form – the *horseshoe can protect you even if you do not believe in its power* – it sums up Casanova's attitude most accurately. It is not that he secretly still believes in its powers but that he is able to activate, produce this 'secret belief' when needed. It is worth noting in this context that, nowadays, magic only really works if you *do not believe in* its powers, and not simply *even if* you do not believe in it. Really superstitious people are constantly frightened and threatened. Superstition does not protect them from anxiety but, rather, generates it; on the other hand, people who do not really believe, or who disavow their belief, appear as 'cool', so that magic seems to be working better for them. This is precisely the difference between superstition and disavowal, or (magical) *belief*.

Casanova does not have a fetish, but one might say that his repeated ritual of fooling others, of inciting and exploiting their gullibility, plays the role of a fetish. Casanova thoroughly *enjoys* arousing a magical belief in others and exposing their gullibility; he enjoys the role of the magician. In doing so – and this emphasis is crucial – he is not looking for a way to believe through others, to perpetuate his own disavowed belief through others (which, according to Mannoni, is the structure of all belief). It might be said, indeed, that we all believe through others (by presupposing some others who naïvely believe), but this is not Casanova's game, which has an additional twist. He is trying to make sure that these others *enjoy their belief*. He enjoys making others believe/enjoy (even if against their will), which is another trait of perversion: enjoyment of enjoyment, doubling of enjoyment, enjoyment in the knowledge of enjoyment. This enjoyment (and my knowledge about it) is also what calls into question the reality of castration (namely: if the other enjoys thanks to my machinations, he/she is not 'castrated'; his/her castration is in my power, under my control, insofar as I can make sure that he/she enjoys). One might thus say that perversion is never merely about the disavowal but about the *enjoyment of the disavowal* – or, more precisely, it is about the disavowal itself becoming the direct source of enjoyment. This is different from the classical structure of disavowal, where the primary aim remains to protect oneself from an unpleasant reality. At the same time, we can see clearly how this redoubling is objectified in the sexual fetish: the fetish allows us not only to ignore a certain reality but also to actively enjoy the tool of this ignoring, the fetish. The fetish acts as a (magical) device for regulating the relationship between desire and enjoyment in their dialectic of 'castration' (where desire is on the side of castration). Perhaps in this case 'disavowing castration' means just that: not that we do not believe in its existence or that we do not 'accept' it, but that we put it on our side, under our control, so that we can use it when necessary. This *usefulness of castration* is also what may explain the following observation by Mannoni, referring to Casanova's story:

> As everyone knows, there is no reason to worry about what the future holds in store for this twenty-three-year-old young man after his cruel ordeal: he makes amends to one and all by performing certain ceremonies that might be called expiatory, relinquishes Genoveffa, and finds himself back where he started from, as full of life as before, and more the magician than ever. There is nothing surprising about this. But we rather frequently encounter similar moments of panic among perverts in analysis; they do not necessarily have a therapeutic effect. Once the panic subsides, there is a return to the status quo.[27]

This, then, would be the difference between Talayesva and Casanova: in what has the structure of a forced choice, Talayesva 'accepts' his own castration in a kind of swop or trade with the Other: he accepts it as a necessary condition of sustaining the castration of the all-enjoying, threatening Other. But he also immediately disavows some aspect of it, and belief gets constituted – this belief is, as it were, genuine.

Casanova's is a different story. It is staged as a direct, open mockery of disavowal (as belief). Casanova claims to *know all about that magic* trick of castration and its trade. Casanova knows how the magic of disavowal works. He is boastingly professing disbelief – that is, attacking the belief (disavowal) itself. But in this he only reinforces, fortifies the disavowal, as becomes clear at the moment of crisis and its inability to really get to him, to change anything.

The lesson we can draw from Casanova's story would thus be the following: it is only by disavowing not just, or simply, the castration but *the form of disavowal itself* (= the belief) that disavowal attaints its 'accomplished' state.

When the crisis is over, Casanova is back to business as usual and nothing really changes. Isn't this also something we often see in the general social response to different crises – namely, the ability to carry on happily without being too shaken by things? And to be proud of this 'resilience' and of our strategies to achieve it? And do we not look down on those who can still be really shaken, anxious, or 'hysterical' by anything in the social (and 'natural') course of events? We forget of course that this resilience mostly exists only in the bubble of our own relationship to ourselves; we forget that there is a storm raging in the real and that we are very likely to be struck by lightning. We are calm not because we have accepted that we have no control over some things anyway but, on the contrary, because we continue to believe that, *thanks to our very disbelief,* we still have control. And that magic can protect us, especially if we don't 'really' believe in it, if we *know better* than to believe it.

3

What about Conspiracy Theories?[1]

There exists a curious complicity between the 'rational' business-as-usual attitude of mainstream society and the 'crazy' attitude of conspiracy theorists. Although the first largely relies on the mechanisms of disavowal whereas the latter comes closer to denial, there is also a certain dialectic that exists between them in their social functioning. Conspiracy theories may be seen as a symptom and an embodiment of the grotesque unconscious of the 'rational elites'. For example: those rational elites 'know' (and say so) that there is climate change, but at the same time they continue with business as usual as if they didn't really believe it. They don't deny climate change, but their everyday business behaviour testifies to their unconscious belief being no different from the explicit denial of conspiracists. At the same time the elites need conspiracy theorists precisely in order to point their finger at them, to contrast the conspiracists' 'craziness' with their own supposed rationality and thus make us blind to their own craziness (which takes the 'rational' form of disavowal, believing that things can more or less remain as they are). In other words, although disavowal and denial are two different concepts, not to be confused with each other, they don't exist in a social vacuum, and the context in which they appear socially can generate a dialectic between them, as is the case in our social and economic context.

In previous chapters, we have been mostly discussing disavowal, so let's now turn our attention to conspiracy theories. The social impact of the latter is growing, and they seem to be moving from the marginal and obscure 'underworld' and subculture to the public space, even into official politics. (The most striking example here is probably the link between QAnon and the politics and person of Donald Trump.) And this certainly calls for an analysis of the social dynamics involved.

At the outset we should identify the element which constitutes a rather direct link between our discussion so far and conspiracy theories, namely the figure of an omnipotent Deceiver. Related to this figure is the feeling of being a mere plaything of the Other, of the Other's enjoyment and satisfaction, which in turn provokes a revolt against it, mostly in the form of revealing and denouncing the evil machinations of the Other. This phenomenon has two sides that are difficult to separate clearly: the side of truth and the side of enjoyment that obscures that same truth.

1. By the side of truth, I mean that the obsession with the enjoyment and machinations of the Other, with its evil and oppressive character, is not only a 'clearly insane' personal pathology; it also has a strong basis in social reality and *its* pathology. Things such as the collapse of social infrastructure, the disintegration of social bonds, precarization, the falling out of (or the impossibility of even entering into) social systems and subsystems by an increasing number of people, the feeling of powerlessness and impotence when it comes to any major decisions that affect our

life, the conviction that others are enjoying at our expense – all these, among others, have led not only or simply to the 'fall of the big Other' but, above all, to its powerful emergence in the form of an Other who is, as it were, obsessed with us. Not because it cares so much about us, but because it wants something from us, because it wants to use and abuse us for its own purposes, which are primarily purposes of enjoyment and power (increasing wealth, control, etc.). Although extremely simplified, this is not simply a false description of the reality of late capitalism, with its almost unimaginable accumulation of wealth and power (decision-making) by a small handful of people, and the cutting off of the vast majority from any serious influence on social and economic developments. One might therefore reasonably ask whether the recent proliferation of conspiracy theories, the rapid spread of conspiracy thinking, is not something of a neurosis of our times – with all the dignity that Freud gave the word when, from the very outset, he recognized its *social* dimension. The resistance to being objects of the Other's satisfaction takes many different forms, including some of the most picturesque and grotesque conspiracy theories. (Followers of QAnon believe, for example, that the world is secretly ruled by a clique of elites – Democrats, Hollywood insiders and billionaires[2] – who worship Satan, indulge in paedophilia, and run a vast trafficking ring in human beings, especially children, whose blood is, among other things, extracted and then grown into plasma, which supposedly prolongs life.)

2. This 'plague of fantasies' is precisely the point where the *truth* (symptom as truth) of social pathology becomes immediately obscured by the surplus enjoyment attached to such fantasies. Conjuring up all possible scenarios of deception and abuse – that is, actively, passionately imagining all the things the Other does to us and to 'our children' – becomes in itself a powerful source of enjoyment and fascination. To some extent at least, this configuration of being at the mercy of a ruthless Other may be related to masochistic perversion, different from sadistic perversion, where the point is to work for the enjoyment of the Other, to put oneself in the role of an instrument (rather than the object) of the Other's enjoyment.

This double play of symptomatic truth and obscurantist will to transform this truth into a means of perverse enjoyment in imagining and replaying all such scenarios of abuse is the reason why, when it comes to conspiracy theories, we might use the paradigm of Lacan's well-known comment on jealousy: even if our partner is actually cheating on us, there is still something pathological about our jealousy; there is a surplus that the 'correspondence with the facts' cannot fully absorb. We might similarly say that, even though some conspiracies really exist, or if they carry in themselves some element of symptomatic truth, there is still something pathological that pertains to conspiracy theories, some surplus investment that is not reducible to these or those facts or truth. On the other hand, it is also important to stress that the 'pathology' at stake here is rarely simply an individual pathology but, rather, registers as a social pathology. As Fredric Jameson argued in his seminal study of conspiracy films of the 1970s and 1980s, conspiratorial thinking often functions as an important means of cognitive mapping in late capitalism – it could be seen as almost the only way left to think about the social as *totality* and about the collective (as opposed to the individual).[3]

Yet our focus here will be not so much on the possible subversive aesthetics of conspiracy theories as on their epistemological passion and its limit – that is, on 'theory' or knowledge. Within a more generalized feeling of anxiety related to (im)possible presentations of social totality, an almost imperceptible shift of emphasis occurs with conspiracy theories: it shifts from the reality described by some ('in truth, the facts are such and such') to the activity of deception. This accounts for the so-called paranoid aspect of conspiracy theories: someone is deliberately manipulating us, doing everything in order not simply to gain from it but to *deceive* us, divert us from how things really stand. There are many shades of this, some of them clearly classifiable as serious pathology, with a reference to 'Them' remaining as the only consistent thread, whereas everything else dissolves into a rather messy bulk. A good example is the following testimony of one of the passionate Flat Earthers who gets the chance to explain his convictions in the Netflix documentary *Behind the Curve*:

And then I found out that it's actually that biblical cosmology is a geocentric cosmology, then I realized why they are hiding the truth. It's because they don't want anyone to know anything. They want people dumb, blind, deaf to the truth, so they can inject you with their vaccines, and their public schooling and this heliocentric model, which is basically forced sun worship.

It soon becomes all about *Them*, who want us to become 'dumb, blind, deaf to the truth', to do and believe what they want. The agent of conspiracy – even if it remains vague and undefined – is in the foreground, omnipresent, and implied in a series of bizarre metonymical shifts concerning the content (vaccinations, public schooling, paganism), the logical connection between which seems clear to the speaker but much less so to the listener (in our case, it seems to be taken randomly from the evangelist repertoire). In this respect, narratives of conspiracy theorists can often strike us as akin to the logic of dreams and the connections established by what Freud called the dream-work: they seem perfectly logical and self-evident to the dreamer, but when the latter wakes up they appear very strange and illogical. And Freud, of course, was right to insist that there *is* nevertheless a logic involved in the dream-work.

Something else about conspiracy theories is interesting and resembles dreams. For the most part, we can say that they do involve or touch some real, or that, with their incredible narratives, they propose a deformed and displaced articulation of something that might be called, following Lacan, *le peu du réel*, a little piece of the real. Let's take the example of a quite popular theory according to which the moon landing was staged in a film studio and never really happened. As Jodi Dean has nicely shown,[4] during the period of the Cold War, the entire American space programme had been intrinsically linked to its own television presentation. The rooting and implementation of TV culture (TV as the new big Other, as a modern focal point, the 'home fire' of every family) had taken place simultaneously and in close relationship with the development of the space programme; from the very outset, the presentation of this programme had been targeting TV audiences, and this included the criteria for choosing and presenting the key protagonists (astronauts) and their families. Could we not

infer from this that television and the moon landing were, in fact, materially bound together in a
kind of surplus overlapping or fusion, and that it
is the real of this fusion that, in a displaced form,
propels and surfaces in theories according to
which the landing never really happened and was
entirely studio staged. This does not mean that
the surplus of TV staging involved in NASA's
moon expedition 'explains' this particular conspiracy theory, or that the latter can be reduced
to it. There are many more things at stake, but
we can say that the investment in its TV staging,
and in the wholesome presentation-production
of the expedition, functions as the 'little piece of
the real' – probably not the only one – at work in
this conspiracy theory.

As already pointed out, conspiracy theories seem to be moving from the marginal and
obscure 'underworld' and subculture to a more
central public space, even official politics. There
are many reasons for this, and they are situated
on many different levels.

For example, one often points the finger at
what appears in our contemporary Western
society as a kind of vulgar and generalized postmodern realization of Nietzscheism: the decline

of objective truth as value and as epistemological category. In this vein, one likes to attribute the fact that 'it is no longer possible to distinguish truth from fiction' to the influence of modern and postmodern theory, to the deconstruction of the notion of the original, to the undermining of different authorities, and to the general promotion of relativism and nominalism ... But, in this enthusiasm of rediscovered realism, one also tends to forget a very realistic fact that it is often quite *objectively* hard – indeed, impossible – to distinguish between the two. Counterfeits and 'fakes' are in fact getting better and better; technology, including AI, has produced some astonishing and disturbing effects in this regard, with things such as artificially generated 'documentary footage' impossible to distinguish from the genuine article. Not to mention that our social relations in late capitalism are excessively fictionalized, in order for the brutal *reality* of capital to be able to follow its course. This is a question not of theory but of real material configurations that include and necessitate such fictions.[5] Postmodern questioning and undermining of the original has long since moved to reality itself and is no longer simply 'a question of perspective', of a theory or an 'ideology' of the multitude of different perspectives.

Another thing that may account for the move of conspiracy theories from the underground to a more central public space appears if we consider the differences between them – that is, different degrees in which they involve and relate to our everyday lives. Flat Earth theory and fake moon landing theory remain mostly abstract mind exercises and are bound more or less exclusively to the idea of Deception. On the other hand, conspiracy theories related to climate change or Covid-19 involve things that affect the everyday practical life of most people. Dealing with these issues demands that we change the way we live and tends to make it more inconvenient. The danger itself remains relatively abstract, whereas dealing with this danger with the premise of preventing it takes very concrete forms, to which we tend to react more directly. Something similar might be said for 'political' conspiracy theories, which respond to what are certainly real problems of real people (economic and social insecurity) by means both of amplifying these insecurities in all kinds of suggestive imaginary ways and of scapegoating (as in the case of the 'great replacement' theory). In other words, and not surprisingly, the rise and 'normalization' of conspiracy theories has its social causes in what appears, in the end, as a normalization of crisis, of crisis as a new way of life.

Common to all kinds of different conspiracy theories – even when politicians officially in power endorse them – is a distrust in the official versions of critical events and their denouncement as 'false'. What prevails in this particular conspiracy form of scepticism is not simply relativism and its proverbial contestation of any ultimate Truth. On the contrary, conspiracists believe that there is Truth; they are just convinced that this truth is different or other than the official one. The paradigmatic idea of conspiracy theories is not that there are many truths (or no truths, just interpretations), but that *there exists another Truth*.

The Subject Supposed to Deceive (Us)

Let's start with the automatic reflex of doubting everything that presents itself as official fact – that is to say, with a principled and pronounced sceptical attitude. Scepticism takes place primarily with respect to symbolic authorities, with respect to 'power', to the supposed self-evidence of general consensus, or simply with respect to everything 'official'. However, and contrary to other critical approaches, conspiracy theories do not busy themselves with analysing the workings of ideology and of 'manufacturing of consent' but immediately jump to what is behind, to hidden depths, to another reality. They never really engage in (critical) analysis of facts and reality in their inner structuring but simply sweep them away as false, and *thus irrelevant*. This basic move from the problematic character of facts and of reality to their resulting *irrelevance* indeed represents – in a quite literal way – the first step towards the 'loss of reality' characteristic of conspiracy theories. The interrogation of why and how illusions appear and structure our reality is immediately solved/dismissed by evoking the Agent of the alleged conspiracy, which 'explains' everything at one stroke. It seems that this Agent of conspiracy, with all the often very complex machinations it is purportedly orchestrating, has only one fundamental agenda: to deceive us, to keep us in error – not so much to deceive us *about* this or that as to deceive us, full stop. It is usually also not very clear why it does this:

deception as such seems to be the main and sufficient motive. Of course, we often get to hear about 'Their interests', 'Their profiting' from it . . . But, these interests and this profit habitually remain rather unclear, abstract, even uncertain, especially if we take into consideration all the incredible effort and expense that would need to be put into deception. Take, for example, the effort (and cost) that would have been needed for 'Them' to sustain the illusion of a round Earth rotating around the sun, if the Earth were, in fact, flat: any possible interest, profit, or gain dissolves in the face of what appears as a much stronger and primordial Interest or Will: to deceive us.

Conspiracy theorists have a very interesting and intricate relationship to what Lacan calls the agency of the big Other. On the one hand, they are convinced that a big Other very much exists (they believe in the existence of an agency which is in itself consistent, operates purposefully, pulls all the strings, and coordinates everything). Yet they also believe that this agency is fundamentally and deliberately evil and deceiving. We might say that they believe in the reality of Descartes' hypothetical evil genius or spirit from the beginning of the *Meditations*, who deliberately deceives us about everything. Could we conclude from this that we are basically dealing with a desperate attempt to preserve the agency of the big Other in the times of its disintegration into a generalized relativism, an attempt that can succeed only at the price of moving the big Other to the zone of malevolence and evil? The consistency of the big Other (its not being 'barred', marked by a lack, as it is in Lacanian theory) can no longer manifest itself in anything else but in the Other successfully deceiving us at all times. A consistent big Other can only be a big Deceiver (a big Fraud or Cheat), an evil Other. A consistent God can only be an evil God; nothing else adds up. Yet better an evil God than no God.

This certainly plays an important part; however, to explain this resurrection of a deceiving Genius by the 'need for a big Other' does not seem to exhaust the phenomenon and the meaning of the assumption shared by all conspiracy theories, namely, that there exists a Subject or Agent who is deliberately deceiving us. The libidinal emphasis is not merely on the existence of the Other (better an evil Other than no Other at all) but also on the implications of this existence *for our being*. If we look at it more closely, we can in

fact see how a (declared) knowledge about a conspiracy intercepts the traumatic certainty-anxiety
of our non-being. It makes it possible to draw the
conclusion that the Other guarantees my being
precisely by trying to systematically deceive me
at all times. Unlike for Descartes, for whom the
activity of deception is not itself an internal condition of *the cogito* (of the certainty of my being),
it now becomes just that: the more the Other tries
to deceive me, the more it is obsessed with me,
the more evident it becomes that I exist. In a way,
this reiterates the *cogito* argument and carries it in
a different direction – or, rather, remains with its
first step, or first certitude, and replays it over and
over again: therefore I am, therefore I am, therefore I am. . . . Descartes argues that, even if all the
thoughts I have are false (induced in me by an evil
genius), the fact remains that I have these (false)
thoughts, therefore I am. This could be directly
transcribed into the 'conspiracy *cogito*' as follows:
I'm being deceived all the time, but I'm the subject of this deception, therefore I am. I'm being
deceived, therefore I am. The deception becomes
necessary for (the question of) my very being.
The question of true or false knowledge (which
for Descartes is at the forefront) disappears into

the background. The important thing is that, as long as there is an attempt to deceive me, as long as I'm an object of the Other's machinations or of the Other's enjoyment, I exist. In this way a conspiracy theory becomes a proof of my existence.

Related to this is another feedback loop of conspiracy theories: their blind spot that appears as their inner limit. If a conspiracy theory turns out to be 'true' and thus becomes the official version of events, this throws a dubious light on the figure of the almighty Deceiver, and hence on our own being. What am I – or am I at all – if there is no more deception? The condition of existence of Conspiracy is, in a way, that it can never really become the official version of events, or else it puts into question my very being. This is why, if something of the conspiracy is officially recognized, it itself immediately provides grounds for further suspicion: maybe this is a new, even more perfidious tactic (a double game) involving a deeper or double level of Conspiracy . . .

Let's imagine for a moment that an objective investigation would, in fact, confirm that the moon landing was staged and filmed in a studio. Would the supporters of this theory be triumphantly opening campaigns, celebrating that their theory prevailed, and that they have been *right* all along? I think it is safe to assume that this would not be the case. This is because what they want to be 'right' about in this whole matter is not the question whether or not man has indeed walked on the moon but the claim that 'They' are systematically deceiving us about that. The moment conspiracy theories turn out to be 'right', they also turn out to be wrong, since the (successful) deception is over and so is the existence of the almighty Deceiver. Even with the most imaginative and bizarre conspiracy narratives the fundamental message is not in their striking content but simply in stressing the dimension of deception and abuse: the belief that the Earth is flat is not really a dispute about the *shape of* the Earth but, rather, an attempt to show that a *massive deception has been systematically taking place* for centuries. This is what the proponents of this theory are trying to prove; the shape of the Earth enters into it more as one of (many possible) examples.

Conspiracy theories can only be right about the authorities systematically and deliberately deceiving us if the deception works fully and is never officially accepted. At least partly related to this is yet another distinctive feature of conspiracy theorists: that they can easily let go of one conspiracy theory and embrace another – that they tend to rotate between different conspiracy theories (often believing in several at once). The emphasis is not so much on the content as on the modality of conspiracy – that is, on the fact that there is a conspiracy going on. What follows from this is that, in their insisting on *another truth*, the emphasis is not in fact so much on truth as it is on 'another', other, different. More exactly, otherness constitutes here an inherent moment of truth; truth is always other (than official) – hence its plasticity and slipperiness. The only truth is that truth is something else.

The Delirium of Interpretation

Related to the preceding is also a specific 'delirium of interpretation' at work in conspiracy theories. Paradoxically, the interpretation is fuelled here by knowledge of the solution, of the end result: the basic question is how to read and interpret what takes place or appears in this world in such a way that we'll get a result given in advance (existing in the basic claims of a conspiracy theory) and which differs from the obvious explanation. In this respect, conspiracy theories resemble what is known from the history of science (particularly astronomy) as 'saving the phenomena' – with the oscillation between the Ptolemaic system and the heliocentric model as the most famous example. The Ptolemaic system, based on the presupposition of the Earth as the centre of the universe, around which other planets circulate, started to be confronted at some point with a growing mass of empirical telescopic observations of planetary movements which did not appear as circular. In response to this, the Ptolemaic astronomers developed a very complex theory of epicycles and eccentric orbits, which would be able to reconcile the observation results with the basic presumption (that the Earth stands motionless and the planets circulate around it) and hence to account for the discordant facts. The heliocentric hypothesis was able to account for these facts better and in a much simpler way, but it required a radical change of the most fundamental cosmological presuppositions. Conspiracy theories often strike one as similar in this practice of 'saving the phenomena': they introduce additional hypotheses and much more complicated explanations of the same events in order to justify their version of reality, which they believe in and take as their starting point.

In addition to the figure of the big Other as the big Deceiver, there exists in some conspiracy theories another instance of a big Other: a big Other that is on our side, a good big Other, the carrier of Truth and Light. This is a feature that brings some of these theories close to religion. The good, truthful Other differs considerably, in its inherent structuring, from the big Other of the consistently deceptive narrative. It does not guarantee our existence, at least not immediately; rather, it guarantees the existence of the all-deceiving Other who in turn guarantees our existence. More precisely even, this other ('good') big Other guarantees, vouches for, our *knowledge* about the deception. It is *the Other supposed to know* about the deception, about the deceiving Other. It functions as a sort of Oracle, as a Grey Eminence of enigmatic messages, which as such do not (yet) form a consistent narrative. It falls to us to construct this Narrative. This is the figure of the good big Other that we encounter, for example, in what is probably the most popular political conspiracy theory today: QAnon.

On 28 October 2017, 'Q' emerged from the primordial swamp of the internet on the message board 4chan and quickly established his legend as a government insider with top security clearance (the co-called Q-clearance) who knew the truth about the secret struggle for power between Trump and the 'deep state'. Since then, he has posted more than 4,000 times. He moved from posting on 4chan to posting on 8chan in November 2017, went silent for several months after 8chan shut down in August 2019, and eventually re-emerged on a new website established by 8chan's owner, 8kun.[6] Though posting anonymously, Q uses a 'trip code' that allows followers to distinguish his posts from those of other anonymous users (known as 'Anons'). Q's posts are cryptic and elliptical, enigmatic. They often consist of a long string of leading questions designed to guide readers towards discovering the 'truth' for themselves through 'research'. The beauty of this procedure is, of course, that, when a concrete prediction fails to come to pass (which happens fairly often), the true believers quickly adapt their narratives to account for inconsistencies. For close followers of QAnon, the posts (or 'drops') contain 'crumbs' of intelligence that they 'bake' into 'proofs'. For 'bakers', QAnon is both a fun hobby and a deadly serious calling.

This particular theory, for which many hold that it is more than a conspiracy theory (a worldview akin to a new religion or a new political movement), thus involves a hierarchical structure, at the centre of which stands 'our' good big Other, fighting from the underground against the evil big Other, who rules the world and keeps us as prisoners of all kinds of illusions. The iconography of resistance movement that stands at the heart of one of the most reactionary conspiracy theories is in itself very interesting and instructive. The movie *The Matrix* presents us with a kind of leftist version of a very similar configuration: a smaller group of freedom fighters is resisting the big Other who keeps the world caught in a gigantic illusion of life and of reality; from the underground the freedom fighters try to break this spell and fight for emancipation. The key figure for the success of this fight is called the Oracle.

In QAnon, Q does indeed function as an oracle: thanks to his supposed access to the highest secrets, he is an embodiment of absolute surplus knowledge, the crumbs of which fall among his followers, who then bake stories out of them – they bake and compose these narratives based on their own research and interpretation. It probably goes without saying that the passion involved in this research provides in itself considerable satisfaction and hence a reward for the bakers' efforts. In some ways, we are dealing with a challenge and a passion similar to that involved in a whole range of games, except that here the lines between game and reality are obliterated from the very outset and the stakes are so much higher. For to be good in this game means to know more about the (true) reality of the world. Besides bakers and the most fervent followers, there is also a big crowd of ordinary believers who simply take these narratives, this *work* (of conspiracy theory) *in progress*, seriously. But also, with these ordinary people, we can detect an unmistakable passion for interpretation, a considerable amount of self-initiative in researching and establishing all kinds of connections, which can also vary considerably – within the general narrative framework of QAnon – depending on the local environment and personal obsessions.

Opposite the big Other as an agent of conspiracy, the big Deceiver thus stands in this conspiracy theory an oracular big Other that calls for interpretation and sustains its delirium; the latter does not tell us the Truth (except, of course, in its vaguest contours), but it helps *us* guess it, dig it out or reconstruct it, fully spell it out by ourselves – and, hence, subjectivize it, take it for our own and, if needed, defend it passionately.

This explains effectively the investment, the zeal that can be observed in conspiracy theorists – including for those conspiracy theories that do not involve any oracular figure and where the enigma consists in putting together different pieces of the world in such a way that they would accord with the utterance describing an alternative reality/truth (a flat Earth, for example).

Belief becomes Knowledge

The truth that we establish based on our own research (and/or deciphering of enigmatic oracular messages) is thus much more strongly subjectivised; one cannot have a neutral, indifferent attitude towards it. It is also much more militantly efficient than a truth simply told or revealed. This is because we spend hours, days,

years looking for and establishing certain connections, moving our knowledge from the register of
supposedly 'better knowledge' to the register of
a considerable cathexis of this knowledge (in the
Freudian sense of *Besetzung*, emotional investment). We are personally invested in it, since it
binds knowledge to our very being.

We also need to pay attention to another
important spin, a circular redoubling that we
can see in many testimonies of fervent followers
of different conspiracy theories. Many emphasize that the first step is not belief. As a rule, it
all starts with disbelief: people hear about some
conspiracy theory and are very sceptical about
it, frequently finding it absurd. Yet something
about it (sometimes its very absurdity) fascinates
them, attracts their attention enough for them to
start looking into it some more, to conduct some
research and – often with fascinated disbelief – to
plunge into the reading of related literature and
websites, which sends them straight down the
rabbit hole. In this process, scepticism and disbelief are gradually replaced by fervent belief in the
knowledge thus obtained – the belief that is all
the more absolute because they have themselves
come to this knowledge, in spite of their original

scepticism, and based on their own research and establishing the right connections.

The scepticism – not just scepticism regarding the official versions of events and official authorities but also the original scepticism concerning the conspiracy theory itself – *is the inherent condition of true belief*, the inherent condition of knowledge and belief becoming One. For this fusion is precisely what takes place here. We are dealing with the following reasoning: 'I knew better (than to believe what this conspiracy theory claims), and this is why I now know that these claims are true.' We can also observe the precise moment where disavowal is situated in this case, the point at which disavowal is in fact involved in the formation of the denial: scepticism (knowing better) plays the role of the shield/disclaimer that allows me first to consider, 'research', and then to accept the opposite of what I know. (I know it sounds ridiculous, but let me nevertheless look into it. . . .) However, disavowal is carried a step further here; it steps out of disavowal at the other end, so to speak. The belief now simply becomes (alternative) *knowledge*. I take what I believe to be *factually true*, whereas perverse disavowal still claims to 'know' that this is not the case. We are no longer dealing with 'I know that this is complete nonsense, but it is still interesting to consider it!'; the split characteristic of the disavowal coagulates into 'I absolutely know' (that this is true).

In this respect, conspiracy theories produce an objectivization of the unconscious knowledge as 'knowledge that doesn't know itself': the unconscious belief is taken to be true knowledge *because it is encountered outside*, because it is not coming from me. It is as if, from the very outset, supporters of a conspiracy theory *knew without knowing*, without knowing that they know. What attracts and fascinates them immediately in a conspiracy theory, in spite of their scepticism, is ultimately that, in a way, 'unconsciously', they already believe, or know: in other words, they encounter their own unconscious as an objective entity, independent of them, floating around in social space. Scepticism (for example: 'I'm not really sure if I can believe there is climate change') thus gets cemented into: 'I always knew there is no climate change', I always-already knew. . . . Our suspicions are objectively confirmed, albeit the objectivity at stake is our own disavowed belief as objectified, and coming from the outside. This goes beyond fetishism and fetishization, in the precise sense that conspiracy theories are like fetishes floating freely in social space, and which we can take for our own or not. If we take them for our own, we discover something that we have ourselves put there, yet paradoxically this something appears to us as the only 'true Outside', a reality such as it is *in itself*, beyond machinations and manipulations of Power (including science). All other objects are just appearances, but this one is singular and renders how things truly are. And whereas a pervert is satisfied by the fetish being just one of appearances (albeit a privileged one), conspiracy theory takes this a step further and, at the same time, exposes the workings of our 'ordinary perversion' based on disavowal. Which is worse? The answer can only be a Leninist one: they are both worse.

4

Conclusion

How, then, would the difference and dialectical relationship between denial as expressed in conspiracy theories and the disavowal discussed in the previous chapters be socially articulated? One feature that stands out is the collective-forming capacity of conspiracy theories. I am not talking about the number of people involved in one or the other. In terms of numbers, disavowal is certainly predominant. As suggested in the Introduction, it also has its social forms and institutions, but this social aspect is not enough to turn it into something like a collective. Perverse disavowal is, so to speak, an individual mass phenomenon. It is the pinnacle of individuality, of individualism, however widespread and in this sense 'universal' it may be. The situation is different with conspiracy theories, which usually coalesce into specific collectives. It may seem paradoxical, but many of these collectives are formed out of an explicit rejection of anything 'collective' (rejection of 'sheep-like' behaviour and existence, as they like to put it). Usually these collectives are labelled with negative terms such as 'mob', 'populist crowd', 'fascist masses'. But since there is nothing even remotely resembling a collective formation on the side of the 'rational' individualist mainstream and its business-as-usual attitude, they will inevitably prevail. Our enlightened Western leaders, who abhor these 'mass formations', have only one response to them: to support and encourage individual levels of disavowal as a means of dealing with crises. This strategy worked for a while but is now failing dramatically because it presupposes a relatively stable social environment with a large and relatively comfortable middle class. Not the kind of serial crisis we are being drawn into.

If Casanova were faced with a new thunderstorm, a new crisis, every other day, we might assume that he too would have been tempted to 'step out of disavowal at the other end'. He might have seized the first fetish floating in social space, a fetish that embodies his unconscious beliefs in a fully spelled out and unrecognizable form as objective knowledge of how things really are. He might become a conspiracy theorist. Bad social circumstances do not necessarily and directly create pathologies or lead to an escalation of atrocities, but they certainly help. The trick, however, is to avoid the condescending attitude of 'understanding', an attitude shared by many on the left, which denies the 'people' any agency other than being a direct expression of their social circumstances – while 'we' can rise above those circumstances and 'understand' those who cannot. As long as crisis is taken to mean 'terrible events happening around us' and our doing our best to cope with them, we remain trapped in the dialectic of repression and in the colourful but no less macabre dance of denial and disavowal. What we really need to understand is not other people ('who are less fortunate or different from ourselves') but the other side of the crisis – i.e., the fact that the other side of the crisis is a scene of continuous, *ongoing struggle*. I'm not simply talking about establishing the true or deeper causes of the crises. A genuine emancipatory struggle is not about establishing the right causality that could ultimately explain (away) these crises. And neither is psychoanalysis. If there is one lesson that social struggles can draw from psychoanalysis, it is the following: *Il n'y a de cause que de ce qui cloche* (Lacan) – there are only causes of what does not work, of what stumbles and points to a gap, a leap, a problem. Emancipatory thinking is not about explaining away the gap and making everything look natural – that is the job of ideology. Emancipatory thinking is about identifying and locating this gap in causality, this glitch, this point of decision where responsibility, agency and, yes, politics come into play. And where things could or should have taken a different direction.

If the ongoing struggle is the other side of crisis, recognizing this and joining the struggle could be an alternative kind of collective-forming action. Joining the struggle does not mean surrendering to the immediacy of the movement that pulls you in. Also, it is not necessary to love your neighbour, or understand her, in order to join a common struggle. It is not even necessary to get rid of all prejudices against them in order to do so. We are trained to jump up and scream at any sign of prejudice and *immediately* to disqualify people who in our view show any of these signs. And that's not a solution, it's part of the problem. To loosen the grip of disavowal and conspiracy thinking, we might need to introduce some alienation and negativity in the midst of all this immediacy. Because that's what both disavowal and conspiracy thinking ultimately thrive on: *Immediacy*. What is being repressed here is the repression, the negativity itself: not simply this or that thing, but the alienating gap that is the armature of repression. The repression of the repression does not make the repression disappear; it only makes it more inaccessible, protected by its own formations. As others have convincingly argued,[1] immediacy is our most treacherous problem: it has permeated all forms of the social and hence has effectively dismantled the social *as a form*.

We began this essay with the dream of a burning child, and with our eagerness to wake up so as not to be exposed to the traumatic aspect of this apparition. Would it be the right answer not to wake up and face it directly, in all its immediacy? No. There is no way to face the trauma directly, and that is what makes it a trauma – something that consumes us and is indistinguishable from the effect it has on us. The more traumatic it is, the more numb we tend to become. We need to wake up – not to forget it and shore up our defences by 'rational means' but, rather, to pursue the trauma and its consequences in the threads and cracks of our normal, everyday reality. The 'true and deeper causes' of crises can only be addressed with attention focused on the surface and the form. Tearing away the veil of the surface, on the other hand, only strengthens the defences and effectively prevents all thinking, struggling and dealing with these causes.

Notes

Introductory Remarks

1 Sigmund Freud, 'Thoughts for the Times on War and Death', in *The Standard Edition of the Complete Psychological Works of Sigmund Freud*, Vol. XIV (London: Vintage Books, 2001), p. 289.

2 Sigmund Freud, 'Fetishism', in *The Standard Edition of the Complete Psychological Works of Sigmund Freud*, Vol. XXI (London: Vintage Books, 2001).

3 Octave Mannoni, 'I Know Well, but All the Same . . .', in *Perversion and the Social Relation*, ed. Molly Anne Rotenberg, Dennis Foster, and Slavoj Žižek (Durham, NC: Duke University Press, 2003).

Chapter 1 Exposition

1 Gérard Wajcman, *Les séries, le monde, la crise, les femmes* (Lagrasse: Verdier, 2018).

2 Sigmund Freud, *The Interpretation of Dreams*, trans. James Strachey, *The Standard Edition of the Complete Psychological Works of Sigmund Freud*, vols IV–V (London: Hogarth Press, 1958), p. 509.

3 Jacques Lacan, *The Four Fundamental Concepts of Psychoanalysis*, trans. Alan Sheridan (New York: W. W. Norton, 1998), p. 59.

4 Jacques Lacan, *Écrits*, trans. Bruce Fink (New York: W. W. Norton, 2006), p. 433.

5 Sigmund Freud, 'Fausse reconaissance (déjà raconté) in psycho-analytic treatment', trans. James Strachey, *The Standard Edition of the Complete Psychological Works of Sigmund Freud*, vol. XIII (London: Hogarth Press 1955), p. 201.

6 Paolo Virno develops this point extensively in his book *Déjà Vu and the End of History* (London: Verso, 2015).

7 Günther Anders, 'Theses for the Atomic Age', *Massachusetts Review* 3/2 (1962): 493–505, at p. 498.

8 See Clément Rosset, *Le réel et son double* (Paris: Gallimard, 1984), p. 91.

Chapter 2 Conceptual Niceties

1 See, for example, Robert Pfaller, *On the Pleasure Principle in Culture: Illusions without Owners* (London: Verso, 2014).

2 Octave Mannoni, 'I Know Well, but All the Same . . .', in *Perversion and the Social Relation*, ed. Molly Anne Rotenberg, Dennis Foster and Slavoj Žižek (Durham, NC: Duke University Press, 2003), p. 70.

3 Sigmund Freud, 'Fetishism', in *The Standard Edition of the Complete Psychological Works of Sigmund Freud*, Vol. XXI (London: Vintage Books, 2001), p. 152.

4 Don C. Talayesva, *Sun Chief: The Autobiography of a Hopi Indian*, ed. Leo W. Simmons (New Haven, CT: Yale University Press, 1942).

5 In his text Mannoni quotes loosely from the French translation of *Sun Chief* (*Soleil Hopi*, trans. Geneviève Mayoux [Paris: Plon, 1959]), p. 84. Since I would first like to present Mannoni's theory, I follow the way he quotes the book in his article.

6 And we do not need to look to ancient societies for examples: admission to various fraternities and sororities, including elite ones, is an example of this in the modern American university environment. The meaning of military service is also often associated with the traumatic incision that turns boys into 'real men' and binds them to the institution of the state.

7 Mannoni, 'I Know Well, but All the Same . . .', p. 71.

8 Sigmund Freud, 'Fixation to Traumas – the Unconscious', *Introductory Lectures on Psychoanalysis* (Harmondsworth: Penguin, 1987), p. 326.

9 Noam Yuran, *The Sexual Economy of Capitalism* (Stanford, CA: Redwood Press, forthcoming).

10 Jacques Lacan, *The Other Side of Psychoanalysis* (New York: W. W. Norton, 2007), p. 82.

11 René Descartes, *Meditations on First Philosophy*, trans. Michael Moriarty (Oxford: Oxford University Press, 2008), pp. 16, 26.

12 Friedrich Nietzsche, *Beyond Good and Evil*, trans. Marion Faber (Oxford: Oxford University Press, 1998), p. 99.

13 In chapter 2, 'The Great Confinement', in *History of Madness* (London: Routledge, 2006).

14 Jacques Lacan, *Le Séminaire, livre XIV: La logique du fantasme* (Paris: Seuil, 2023). I'm also relying on Jacques-Alain Miller's reading of it in his 1984/85 course *1, 2, 3, 4* (unpublished).

15 Jacques Lacan, *The Four Fundamental Concepts of Psychoanalysis*, trans. Alan Sheridan (New York: W. W. Norton, 1998), p. 224.

16 Alain Grosrichard, 'Une expérience psychologique au dix-huitième siècle', *Cahiers pour l'Analyse* 2: 104.

17 Lacan, *La logique du fantasme*, p. 93.

18 Ibid., p. 72.

19 I'm borrowing the wording from Miller's *1, 2, 3, 4*, course of April 24, 1985.

20 Jacques Lacan, *Le Séminaire, livre X: L'angoisse* (Paris: Seuil, 2004), p. 92.

21 Sigmund Freud, *Totem and Taboo* and *Other Works*, trans. James Strachey, *The Standard Edition of the Complete Psychological Works of Sigmund Freud*, Vol. XIII (London: Hogarth Press, 1955).

22 Here I refer to Mohamed Tal's *The End of Analysis: The Dialectics of Symbolic and Real* (Cham: Palgrave Macmillan, 2023), p. 56.

23 Ibid.

24 Slavoj Žižek, *In Defense of Lost Causes* (New York: Verso, 2008), p. 299.

25 Giacomo Casanova, *History of My Life*, trans. Willard R. Trask (Baltimore: Johns Hopkins University Press, 1997).

26 Quoted in Mannoni, 'I Know Well, but All the Same . . .', p. 86.

27 Ibid., p. 87.

Chapter 3 What about Conspiracy Theories?

1 This chapter reiterates some of the arguments that I developed in a longer text on conspiracy theories. See Alenka Zupančič, 'Short Essay on Conspiracy Theories', in Adrian Johnston, Boštjan Nedoh, and Alenka Zupančič, eds, *Objective Fictions* (Edinburgh: Edinburgh University Press, 2022).

2 Here are some of the names that keep coming up: Hillary Clinton, Barack Obama, George Soros, Bill Gates, Tom Hanks, Oprah Winfrey, Chrissy Teigen, and Pope Francis.

3 Fredric Jameson, *The Geopolitical Aesthetic: Cinema and Space in the World System* (Bloomington: Indiana University Press, 1992).

4 Jodi Dean, *Aliens in America: Conspiracy Cultures from Outerspace to Cyberspace* (New York: Cornell University Press, 1998).

5 See Slavoj Žižek's analysis in the section 'Fiction and/in Reality' of his *Surplus-Enjoyment: A Guide for the Non-Perplexed* (London: Bloomsbury, 2022).

6 Julia Carrie Wong, 'QAnon Explained: The Antisemitic Conspiracy Theory Gaining Traction around the

World', *The Guardian*, 25 August 2020; www.theguar
dian.com/us-news/2020/aug/25/qanon-conspiracy-
theory-explained-trump-what-is.

Conclusion

1   See Anna Kornbluh, *Immediacy, or, The Style of Too
Late Capitalism* (London: Verso, 2023).